C000140666

EUROPEAN CASH MANAGEMENT
— A GUIDE TO BEST PRACTICE

EUROPEAN CASH MANAGEMENT — A GUIDE TO BEST PRACTICE

Marie Dolfe and Anna Koritz

JOHN WILEY & SONS, LTD

Chichester · New York · Weinheim · Brisbane · Singapore · Toronto

Copyright © 1999 by   John Wiley & Sons Ltd,
Baffins Lane, Chichester,
West Sussex PO19 1UD, England
National   01243 779777
International (+44) 1243 779777
e-mail (for orders and customer service enquiries):
cs-books@wiley.co.uk
Visit our Home Page on http://www.wiley.co.uk
or http://www.wiley.com

All Rights Reserved. No part of this publication may be reproduced, stored in a retrieval system, or transmitted, in any form or by any means, electronic, mechanical, photocopying, recording, scanning or otherwise, except under the terms of the Copyright, Designs and Patents Act 1988 or under the terms of a licence issued by the Copyright Licensing Agency, 90 Tottenham Court Road, London, UK W1P 9HE, without the permission in writing of the publisher.

Marie Dolfe and Anna Koritz have asserted their right under the Copyright, Designs and Patents Act 1988, to be identified as the authors of this work.

Other Wiley Editorial Offices

John Wiley & Sons, Inc., 605 Third Avenue,
New York, NY 10158-0012, USA

WILEY-VCH Verlag GmbH, Pappelallee 3,
D-69469 Weinheim, Germany

Jacaranda Wiley Ltd, 33 Park Road, Milton,
Queensland 4064, Australia

John Wiley & Sons (Asia) Pte Ltd, 2 Clementi Loop #02-01,
Jin Xing Distripark, Singapore 129809

John Wiley & Sons (Canada) Ltd, 22 Worcester Road,
Rexdale, Ontario M9W 1L1, Canada

Library of Congress Cataloging-in-Publication Data

Dolfe, Marie.
    European cash management / Marie Dolfe and Anna Koritz.
    p. cm.
    Includes bibliographical references and index.
    ISBN 0-471-86550-8 (alk. paper)
    1. Cash management—Europe.   I. Koritz, Anna.   II. Title.
    HG4028.C45D65   1999
    658.15'244—dc21   99–40031
                                                              CIP

British Library Cataloguing in Publication Data

A catalogue record for this book is available from the British Library

ISBN 0-471-86550-8

Typeset in 11/14pt Palatino by Mackreth Media Services, Hemel Hempstead, Herts.
Printed and bound in Great Britain by Bookcraft (Bath) Ltd, Midsomer Norton, Somerset.
This book is printed on acid-free paper responsibly manufactured from sustainable forestry, in which at least two trees are planted for each one used for paper production.

CONTENTS

PREFACE

Technological advances are currently more rapid than ever. This impacts modern cash management in two main ways. First, it forces every business to be prepared for rapid investment or divestment decisions at all times. This makes it more important than ever for the corporation to ensure it has absolute control over its cash position and other liquid assets. Recent years have seen an ever-increasing escalation in merger and acquisition activity across Europe. A modern, streamlined infrastructure for European cash management facilitates rapid and efficient integration of new entities into the larger group and enables the corporation to obtain intended synergy effects as rapidly as possible.

The second impact of the technological advances are the possibilities offered to replace old and inefficient cash management practice with modern processes taking full advantage of the latest tools available to cash and treasury management. Whilst many corporations in Europe have already made the investment to upgrade their cash management infrastructures to modern best practice, a surprisingly large number of important corporations still maintain out of date and inefficient practice.

Our ambition is that this book will provide ideas and input for every category of corporation active in Europe. Certain parts of the book treat the fundamentals of good cash management, whilst other parts go into more advanced best practice.

We have primarily based this handbook on our personal experiences made working with a large number of international corporations and banks in Europe. However, we would like to express our sincere gratitude to a number of people who have provided valuable help and advice. We thank Kai Barvell, Director of the Payment Systems Department at the Central Bank of Sweden, for valuable advice on how best to describe the new European clearing infrastructures. For input as to the banker's view of international payments and clearing, we thank Roger Storm, Head of Trade Services Products of S E B and Bo Thulin, Head of Cash Management of Merita Nordbanken Sweden. We are also grateful to the various corporations who have given us their permission to describe their cash management solutions as case studies in the book. We further wish to thank our colleagues Mary Ann

Dowling, Ernst & Young New York and Coen Kranenberg, Ernst & Young Amsterdam, as well as our colleagues at Ernst & Young Stockholm, Staffan Ekström, Stefan Lambert and Karin Sancho for their generous advice, comments and contributions. Last but foremost, we would like to thank our colleagues Anette Karlsson, whose experience and previous work[1] in the area of cash inflow and outflow processes have provided important input to chapters 3 and 4, and Lars Weigl, without whose support and encouragement inspiration this book would have never been completed.

Marie Dolfe, Vienna, and Anna Koritz, Stockholm, 1999

---

1   Previously published in Swedish: Att tjäna pengar på pengar — Cash Management, by Anette Karlsson, Ernst & Young Skriftserie Nr 31/96, 2nd revised edition.

WHAT IS CASH MANAGEMENT AND WHY IS IT IMPORTANT?

INTRODUCTION

In this book, we will describe various techniques for working effectively with cash management and particularly with international cash management. But, before entering into the details, let us define what we mean by cash management and why it is important for the short and long term success of each corporation. In this chapter, we will describe how cash management has a direct impact on your company's shareholder value and on its profitability. Remember, cash management will impact these important measures regardless of whether you actively manage your cash or not! The difference is, active and efficient cash management will have a positive impact on shareholder value and profitability, while negligent or inefficient cash management will have a directly negative impact.

DEFINITION OF CASH MANAGEMENT

There are many different ways to define *cash management*. One definition is: "Making money on money". That is a correct definition, but we think it should be expanded to include "...and making money on efficient procedures and support systems."

Cash management should be proactive and flexible, aiming at releasing capital employed from your balance sheet and improving your financial net, whilst identifying and realising administrative cost savings.

The scope and boundaries of cash management varies between different countries and companies. This is how we usually describe the scope of cash management.

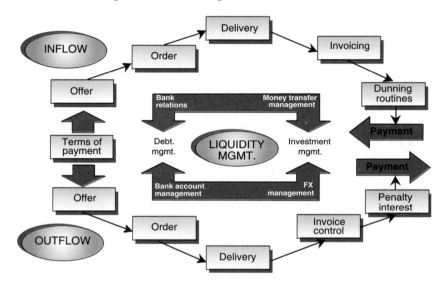

Cash management model

This model can be viewed in three main parts: Inflow of cash, Outflow of cash and Liquidity management.

- Inflow of cash starts with the customer order and is completed when customer payment is received.
- Symmetrically, outflow of cash starts with placing an order and is completed when payment has been made.
- Liquidity management covers liquidity forecasting, short term funding and investments, foreign exchange as well as bank account and bank relationship management.

Chapters 3 and 4 will briefly cover the areas of inflow and outflow of cash, whilst the majority of the book will focus on the area of liquidity management.

Sometimes the management of physical goods and stock is also considered a part of cash management. We prefer to refer to that as *working capital management*. These areas will not be covered in this book.

WHY CASH MANAGEMENT IS IMPORTANT

Cash management and value based management

Each company should aim to optimise the shareholder value. This means maximising the value of their long term share price by understanding and measuring performance using market values, rather than traditional accounting based performance measures.

So, how is shareholder value built? Consider this illustration:

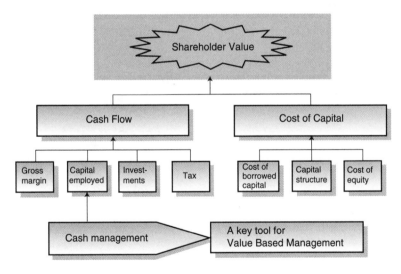

Shareholder value

The shareholder value is equal to the net present value of all future cash flow of the company. The net present value of the cash flow is simply the sum of all the future cash flow streams, discounted with the cost of capital. The cash flow is a function of the gross margin, investments, tax and *changes to the capital employed*.

With cash management you can directly impact the amount of capital employed. Thus, cash management is one of the key tools for *Value Based Management*.

Cash management and profitability

The traditional measure of the success of a company is *profitability*. We will now show you how cash management has a direct impact on profitability.

Profitability can be described as follows:

$$\text{Profitability} = \frac{\text{Profit}}{\text{Assets}}$$

$$= \frac{\text{Profit}}{\text{Assets}} \times \frac{\text{Turnover}}{\text{Turnover}}$$

$$= \frac{\text{Profit}}{\text{Turnover}} \times \frac{\text{Turnover}}{\text{Assets}}$$

$$= \text{Profit margin} \times \text{capital turnover rate}$$

Profitability is the measure of the company's profit in proportion to the assets invested. Using simple algebra, we can multiply the nominator and the denominator with the same parameter, turnover, without changing the value of the expression. This allows us to show that profitability can also be described as the product of the profit margin, i.e. the profit relative to the turnover, and the capital turnover rate, i.e. the turnover as a proportion of the assets. Good cash management will improve the profit margin as well as the capital turnover rate. Thus, cash management will have an immediate effect on your profitability.

This can also be illustrated with the following diagram:

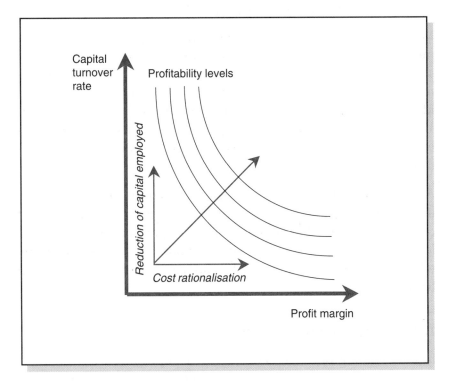

Profitability levels

Increasing the capital turnover ratio means releasing cash from the balance sheet. The capital which is released can be used for dividends, investments or for repaying debts. This will lead to interest savings. By improving the speed with which you receive payments, by keeping your money as long as you can without incurring cost and through efficient liquidity management you will increase the capital turnover ratio of your company and, thus, move upwards in the diagram above and reach higher profitability levels. Through cost efficient administrative procedures and by minimising your cost for bank services, you will move to the right in the diagram, to higher profitability levels.

A CASH MANAGEMENT STUDY

Most companies benefit from performing regular cash management studies. A cash management study focuses on a detailed study of all processes which are relevant to the cash management performance of the company. This is an efficient way to identify cash management savings opportunities. A cash management study identifies float savings and bank fee savings as well as savings through more efficient administrative procedures.

At the same time, all personnel involved in these processes increase their awareness of the importance and nature of efficient cash management behaviour. This is important for ensuring a long term effect of the study. The methodology we usually apply when performing a typical cash management study is described below.

1. Planning and preparations

In the planning phase, it is decided which persons are to be interviewed during the study. Interviews should be performed with all those employees which hold positions that significantly impact the cash management of the company. The number of interviews will vary depending on the type of company and on how the business is organised.

A brief questionnaire will be sent out to each person who is to be interviewed, in order that they may get a chance to prepare for the interview.

2. On site study

Information is gathered at each relevant site through interviews, samples and analysis of reports or figures already available.

The interview phase is always started by information meetings for all employees which are concerned. The information meeting usually contains an introduction to cash management and a presentation of the different steps of the cash management study.

3. Analysis, quantification of savings and development of a report

In the project report, a systematic analysis of the cash management activities of the company is presented, area by area. In the analysis, the cash management model presented on page 2 is followed. The quantification of savings opportunities is presented in an easy to follow manner, so that every reader can assess the benefit of implementing the recommendation. The report also contains a suggested implementation plan for the savings which have been identified.

4. Presentation of the report

When the analysis and the report are completed, the project team first presents their conclusions and recommendations to the management team of the company, or an appointed steering committee. Thereafter, a presentation is made to all concerned employees.

5. Implementation

The project report should be shaped so that the report and the contained implementation plan can support the implementation of the accepted recommendations. Sometimes, a more detailed implementation plan also needs to be developed, with clear allocation of responsibilities and deadlines related to each task involved.

In order to ensure that the study has provided the benefits expected, we always recommend that a follow-up study should be performed 6–12 months after the initial cash management study.

The benefits of a cash management study

The result of a cash management study performed with this methodology can be summarised as follows:

- Systematic evaluation and documentation of existing procedures in accordance with the cash management model presented above on page 2.
- Practical recommendations for improved cash inflow, cash outflow and liquidity management processes, resulting in cost savings as well as reduction of capital employed which brings interest savings.
- Increased awareness and knowledge in the company as regards:
  —the importance of capital employed on shareholder value and profitability and that time means money
  —how each individual can contribute to the reduction of capital employed by thinking and acting cash management in executing his/her daily tasks.

THE FOLLOWING CHAPTERS

The purpose of this book is to function as a practical handbook in cash management for anyone studying or managing corporate cash management as well as for bankers providing cash management services to corporate customers.

In the next chapter, you can read about current trends in cash management. Where is cash management going and which development aspects should we keep in mind when shaping current cash management solutions which we don't want to become obsolete over night?

The subsequent two chapters, chapters 3 and 4, take you through the fundamentals of corporate cash management. Chapter 3 discusses the inflow of funds to a corporation. In chapter 4, you can read about the outflow of funds. We hope every reader will receive some helpful hints of how to find improvement opportunities in these fundamental, but important, cash management processes. The reader who is already experienced in corporate cash management may choose to skip these chapters and go directly on to the more advanced areas of clearing, payments, receipts and liquidity management, where more development has occurred in recent times.

Clearing, payments and receipts are topics which are developed in chapter 5. Whilst not going into specifics of each European clearing system or payment method, the major concepts of clearing should be understood after reading this chapter and the reader will be familiar with the most common payment and receipt methods available in modern cash management.

The following four chapters deal with liquidity management related topics. The first of these chapters, chapter 6, provides an introduction to cash pooling and describes the three major European methods of pooling, which are zero balance pooling, notional pooling and single legal account pooling. The functionality as well as advantages and disadvantages of these concepts are described.

In chapter 7, we discuss how you can utilise the basic concepts of cash pooling to structure efficient bank account management. Primarily, an international situation is considered. Various strategies are investigated, from the "complete independence of subsidiaries" strategy to the "single bank concept".

Chapter 8 treats the highly relevant topic of active liquidity management. How can we find ways to effectively forecast and manage our international liquidity?

The last two chapters cover the selection and procurement of bank services and the successful implementation of these. Chapter 9 provides helpful hints and checklists for the entire selection process, from fact finding and visioning to the completion of the bank selection.

In chapter 10, we share some practical experience from the implementation of bank services. The implementation of a new cash management concept can be a major and expensive investment and should be undertaken with as much professionalism as possible. This chapter aims to provide some practical suggestions for anyone about to enter such a venture.

We hope you will enjoy our book and take something with you for your day-to-day practical benefit.

2

TRENDS IN CASH MANAGEMENT

INTRODUCTION

The area of cash management is becoming increasingly interesting as the technological and geographical possibilities for balance sheet improvement and efficiency enhancement continue to offer new and exciting opportunities. The introduction of the Euro has opened unprecedented routes to efficient cash management in Europe. Simultaneously, technological advances pave the way for new solutions. In fact, the selection of cash management bank services increasingly resembles the selection of software solutions.

In this chapter, we will briefly touch on a number of trends which we believe are currently heavily influencing the development of the cash management area. These are:

- The consolidation of bank relationships
- Euro cash pooling
- Shared service centres
- Electronic data interchange
  - The standardisation of electronic banking platforms
  - The development of bank neutral electronic platforms
- Outsourcing
- Internet

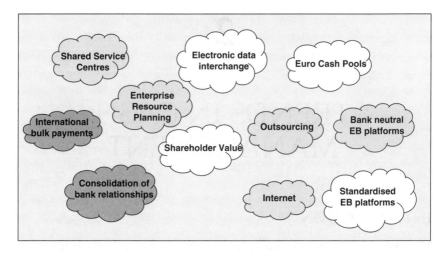

Trends in cash management

CONSOLIDATION OF BANK RELATIONSHIPS

There is currently a strong trend towards consolidation of the bank relationships of multinational corporations. This trend is supported from two angles.

1. On the banking side, the European Monetary Union increases the competition for providing payment services by allowing foreign banks access to previously relatively protected regions. The keys to profitability in the low margin business of payment services are volume and the capability to invest in efficient technological platforms. Therefore, the pressure for mergers and acquisitions in the banking sector is, and will continue to be, high. Consequently, the number of eligible banks is decreasing.

2. On the corporate side, new technological advances allow multinational corporations to implement streamlined IT platforms throughout their business, using so called *Enterprise Resource Planning (ERP) systems*. Apart from enabling improved information management, this can also bring tremendous efficiencies in terms of IT maintenance and support. Therefore, increasingly, corporations question why they

need to interface their streamlined account payable and receivable ledgers to different banking platforms in each European country. A corporate demand has grown for one streamlined cash management interface to the bank across Europe. Most financially independent corporations decrease their number of cash management bank relationships in Europe today.

EURO CASH POOLING

The introduction of the Euro enables the netting of positive and negative cash balances across the Euro zone. This enables unprecedented balance sheet improvements, which are followed by the corresponding reduction of interest cost. Also, this is an enabler for more efficient liquidity management. Now, the treasurer of an international corporation has one instead of 11 currencies to manage each day. Of course, this is a strong driver for centralising treasury management, as the saving is hardly of the same magnitude if you keep a local treasurer to manage the Euros in each country.

Last, but importantly, Euro pooling concentrates more of your cash management business to each bank. The increased volume will improve your negotiating position when agreeing terms and conditions with the bank. Corporations which have already entered these relationships have found they have realised significant cuts in fees and float, whilst improving interest spread conditions and service levels.

SHARED SERVICE CENTRES

What is it?

Around 1985, the first large US corporations started organising their support processes in shared service centres. In 1995, these companies brought the concept to Europe. Today, a large proportion of European corporations have already implemented or are investigating the opportunities to benefit from this concept.

A shared service centre is a shared unit within the corporation, serving a number of different business units. Ideally, the service centre is owned and managed by the participating business units. The service provided is regulated in service level agreements between the service centre and the business units. Participation in the service centre should be voluntary, thereby encouraging competition with other alternatives and promoting top quality services from the service centre. The service centre will reach the critical mass to provide a centre of excellence for service and to invest in up to date technology and realise economies of scale. Primarily, though, the use of a shared service centre will off-load the business units from their administrative or logistic burden and enable these units to fully focus on their core business, which is usually sales or production.

Why is this relevant to cash management?

The emergence of shared service centres has triggered the development of new bank products, designed to serve shared service centres. Two processes, frequently operated in pan-European shared service centres, are the payment and receipt processes. Several banks have developed products which enable the disbursement of commercial domestic bulk payments to be made from one geographical point in Europe, but still be processed through local clearing throughout Europe. This is what we usually refer to as *international bulk payments*.

Another product, which is widely known in the US, is the lockbox. The lockbox tool is now becoming increasingly well known in Europe, as an enabler to the remote collection of paper based payments in shared service centres.

Furthermore, not only corporations but also many banks have adopted the shared service concept as an important enabler to achieving economies of scale in transaction processing. With the US based banks as forerunners, most European banks have either started shared service centre activities or are investigating such opportunities.

ELECTRONIC BANKING

Standardisation

European electronic banking (EB) platforms are increasingly harmonised. Most EB platforms can now be used for domestic as well as international payments. Whilst most countries still have bank specific platforms, i.e. you need to install one EB platform per cash management bank, certain countries, such as Germany, have managed to agree on one common EB platform — in the German case called Multicash. This standard is now spreading into the Eastern European markets.

The use of EB platforms is becoming increasingly sophisticated. Modern cash management requires that the corporation integrates its systems with the EB platform. Interfaces are developed for generating automatic payment and direct debit instructions, but also for automatic upload of transaction statements for automatic reconciliation of payments, receipts and account balances.

As the development of customised interfaces is expensive, many banks are now marketing standardised interfaces to the major Enterprise Resource Planning systems, such as SAP and Oracle.

Bank neutral EB platforms

The concentration of bank relationships is considered by certain corporations to be a risk. A small number of cash management banks along with highly and expensively integrated systems bring on an exposure to those relationships that some companies wish to avoid. Therefore, a number of bank neutral EB platforms have emerged on the market. These EB platforms are integrated to the corporations core systems. The bank neutral EB platform is prepared for standardised integration with banks. Thus, you can relatively easily change banks whilst maintaining a high degree of integration, without rebuilding customised bank specific interfaces.

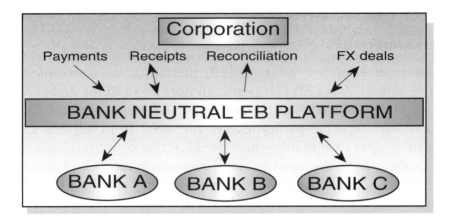

Bank neutral integration

Electronic Data Interchange

Electronic data interchange (EDI) is an established form of communication between corporations, particularly as regards logistics. Financial EDI, the interchange of electronic financial messages such as invoices or payment orders, have also existed, primarily in the US, for a number of years. However, the growth of financial EDI in Europe has been slow. This has mainly been due to a lack of commonly accepted standards. Now, EDIFACT appears to be winning the battle of the standards and, although EDIFACT messages, too, show variations, this is now increasingly to be found as the standard for payment related messages.

This is changing the character of services sought from banks by leading corporations. Increasingly, it is the delivery of standardised financial messages, rather than simply the transfer of funds, which is expected as part of the payment service. The sophisticated customer expects to be able to electronically dispatch the remittance advice along with the payment. The same type of customers will also expect to be able to receive information from their banks allowing automated reconciliation of their receivables and payables ledgers.

OUTSOURCING

Another strong movement at the moment is outsourcing. Some examples of cash management related functions which are increasingly outsourced are:

- Printing of invoices, cheques etc.
- Receivables reconciliation
- Treasury functions, such as hedging, liquidity management, back-office functions etc.

There are many different reasons why a corporation may choose to outsource any of these functions. First and foremost, the reason that this is happening now is that it is only in the last few years that an efficient supply of outsourcing services has emerged. Why, then, has this supply emerged? Primarily, we believe, because there are now technological solutions, such as reliable network technology, workflow and imaging, which allow for efficient out-sourcing alternatives to be developed. Other reasons are:

- Balance sheet improvements
- Cost reduction
- A desire to focus on the core business
- Insufficient expertise
- Economies of scale
- Space or other resource constraints

Certain banks have grasped this opportunity to develop new business with their existing customers and now offer outsourcing services. The border-line of which part of the cash management services are performed by the bank and which are performed by the corporation is no longer as clear cut as it used to be.

INTERNET

The explosion of internet use has not left the financial markets unaffected. Already, the internet is an established sales channel for Financial Supermarkets, i.e. banks and insurance companies which offer home shopping of their services on the internet.

Many European banks offer their customers the ability to pay their bills and view their bank account details directly on the internet. So far, these offers are primarily directed to and used by consumers. However, products for corporate cash management are starting to emerge and many banks are already converting their EB systems to internet based technology solutions. This, we expect, will be the first step to the new technological cash management environment.

CONCLUSION

So, are these developments unrelated? No, hardly.

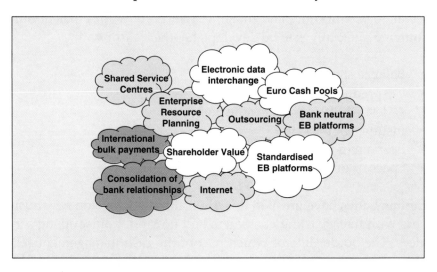

Technical integration and economies of scale for shareholder value

One way or another, most current trends in cash management evolve around two themes: *Technical integration* and *economies of scale*, which are utilised to increase the shareholder value.

Technical integration is directly relevant to the ERP, Internet, EB platform, Euro cash pool and EDI trends, just to mention a few. Economies of scale characterise shared service centres, euro cash pooling, international bulk payments, outsourcing and several other of the current cash management trends.

In fact, not only do all these trends emanate from the same basic concepts. They are also heavily inter dependant. For example, the explosion of the ERP systems have contributed to strengthen the trend for consolidation of bank relationships and also the growth of the shared service centre concept.

3

THE INFLOW OF FUNDS TO THE CORPORATION

INTRODUCTION

Whilst the majority of this book will concentrate on the most complex part of modern cash management, the liquidity management process, this chapter and the next provide some fundamental insight in the cash receipt and cash payment processes. A focused study of these processes which exist in every business, usually reveals significant savings opportunities. Savings can normally be identified as regards the reduction of capital employed as well as efficiency gains.

Accounts receivable can be considered as money which belongs to the selling company but is held by its customers. The selling company usually carries the cost of that capital as well as the risk. In most business activities, a significant part of the capital employed consists of accounts receivable.

The credit which the customer is granted can be considered as a loan to the customer. To reduce the cost and the risk of these loans, the accounts receivable should be kept as low a possible.

The credit arrow

The below illustration describes the major events which take place during the time in which capital is tied up in accounts receivable. We call this a credit arrow.

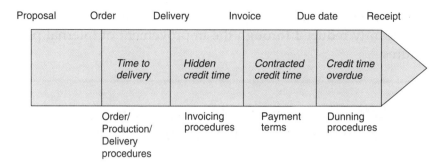

Credit arrow

The total credit time is the lead time between delivery and the receipt of payment. It is important to keep the total credit time as short as possible to avoid capital being tied up in accounts receivable. The total credit time can, as illustrated above, be divided into the hidden credit time, the contracted credit time and the credit time overdue.

Hidden credit time

Hidden credit time, i.e. the time from delivery of goods or services to invoicing, exists in most lines of business. This is the credit time which is often the most difficult to manage, as it can usually not be retrieved from the companies information systems. All hidden credit time should be eliminated through the introduction of more efficient procedures for better, complete and more rapid communication between the sales function and the invoicing function.

Credit time overdue

Credit time overdue is the time between the invoice due date and the receipt of payment. Late customer payments are often directly or indirectly caused by the selling company. For example, the proposal or the invoice may contain unclear instructions, the invoice may have been sent to the wrong address or the selling company may have insufficient dunning procedures.* Therefore, the average credit time overdue can often be significantly reduced through the improvement of internal procedures.

> **Late customer payments are often directly or indirectly caused by the selling company!**

Customer relationship

The management of accounts receivable is an important part of the customer relationship. Professional procedures in this area contribute to the customer developing a positive view of the selling company.

> **The management of accounts receivable is an important part of the customer relationship**

In order to shorten the credit arrow and thereby reduce capital employed, everyone involved within the company must participate. Everybody must strive in the same direction for results to be obtained!

Analysis

In order to establish which are the time lags and how much money can be saved in the cash receipt process you should follow a number of actual transactions from proposal to final receipt of cash. If

---

*   See further on pages 39–44.

unnecessary delays are identified between the different steps in the process, a more detailed investigation of the concerned procedures should be performed and more efficient procedures should be designed and implemented in order to avoid unnecessary time lags.

In the next few sections, the cash receipt process is described step by step, from proposal to final receipt of cash. The description can be used as a check list for analysis of your company's cash receipt process. The different steps of the cash receipt process are illustrated by the arrow below.

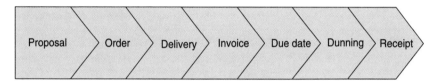

The cash receipt process

PROPOSAL

An important aspect of cash management is the quality of documentation. It is important that each document exchanged between a selling party and its customer contains relevant and consistent information. This is pertinent to all documentation, from the proposal and order confirmation to the invoice and possible payment reminders.

It is at the proposal stage that your ability to impact the duration of the credit time is created. Therefore, it is important to pay attention to the following aspects when submitting a proposal.

Credit and payment terms

Always try to avoid long credit terms, even if the customer would be prepared to pay for credit! A longer credit term generally increases your risk, as the credit worthiness of the customer may deteriorate before payment is made.

Whenever adjusting a credit term, the resulting profit or loss must be considered. When the credit term is extended, an adjustment of the price should be considered as a compensation for the increased cost of interest and the higher credit risk.

The payment term in the proposal should state that if a query arises regarding any part of the invoice, that part of the invoice which is not object to the query should be paid on the due date.

Normal credit terms

Austria	30–60 days net
Belgium	30–60 days net
Denmark	Domestic: 30 days Export: 60 days
Finland	14 days 30 days (against interest compensation) 60 days (export)
France	30–90 days net Free delivery month standard practise
Germany	30 days
Great Britain	Domestic: 30 days Export: 30–90 days
Iceland	30–60 days
Italy	60–90 days 30 days 50%, the rest 60 days
Norway	15–30 days net
Spain	30–90 days net
Sweden	30 days
Switzerland	30–90 days
The Netherlands	30 days
The United States	30 days

Source: Intrum Justitia International AB

Cash discounts

Cash discounts are usually unprofitable for the selling company and should, if possible, be avoided. For example, proposing "10 days −2,5%, 30 days from invoice date net" is equivalent to borrowing money at a yearly interest rate of 45%[1]. In reality, the cost is probably even higher, as the customer often pays after 30 days or later, but still deducts the cash discount. Recovering incorrectly claimed cash discounts can be very difficult. The table below provides you with the equivalent yearly interest as expressed in cash discount terms.

Cash discount key–Annualised interest rate

Cash discount	Days				
	10	15	20	30	45
1%	36%	24%	18%	12%	8%
1.5%	54%	36%	27%	18%	12%
2%	72%	48%	36%	24%	16%
2.5%	90%	60%	45%	30%	20%
3%	108%	72%	54%	36%	24%
3.5%	126%	84%	63%	42%	28%

---

1   Some companies consider cash discounts in a different way. They think of the price minus the cash discount as the actual list price, and consider the cash discount rather to be a penalty interest to be paid by those customers which are prepared to pay for long credit terms. Under such circumstances, the cash discount can be considered to be an enabler to efficient cash management.

Example:
What is the equivalent interest per year, if the cash discount offered is "15 days −2% cash discount, 30 days net from invoice date"?
The cost of receiving the payment 15 days earlier (30–15) is 2%.
Go to the table row 2% and the column 15 days.
Result = 48% interest per year.
Offering cash discounts is very expensive for the selling company!

Cash discount practises

Austria	8–14 days, 2–3%
Belgium	10 days, 2%
Denmark	Unusual. Certain industries: 10 days, 2–3%
Finland	14 days, 2%
France	Cash payment, 1–2.5%
Germany	Usual in certain industries, e.g. textile: 10 days, 3%
Great Britain	Unusual, only exists in certain industries
Iceland	Immediate payment, 5–7%
Italy	Unusual but negotiable. Depends on the product and the size of the amount.
Norway	Unusual, only exists in certain industries. 10 days, 2%
Spain	Unusual
Sweden	Unusual, only exists in certain industries.
Switzerland	5 days, 2%
The Netherlands	Only exists in a few industries. 10 days, 2%
The United States	10 days, 2%

Source: Intrum Justitia International AB

Payment instructions

The proposal, or possibly the terms of purchase attached to the proposal, should contain instructions on the preferred means of payment. Incoming funds should reach an interest bearing bank account as soon as possible. Thus, you need to minimise the time lag from the point where the customer makes the payment, the money arrives at your bank, is posted to your account and, most importantly, is given value by the bank, i.e. starts to earn interest. The most efficient means of payment will vary between different countries and will depend on your contract with your bank. Usually, electronic transfers are the most efficient means of payment, but you need to investigate this case by case. Read more about value dating in Chapter 5: *Clearing, payments and receipts.*

Customers which choose to use a different payment method than the one you state in the proposal, terms of purchase or invoice should be contacted and urged to change payment method.

When the customer makes regular payments to the selling party, it may be advantageous to consider using direct debits. Direct debit means that money is transferred on your instruction from your customer's account to your own on the due date.

The advantages of direct debit for the selling company are:

- Payment is made on the due date.
- Short term cash flow forecasting becomes more accurate.
- Credit time overdue decreases.
- The number of reminder letters required is reduced.
- May simplify reconciliation, depending of the functionality of the accounts receivable ledger.

The advantages of direct debit for the customer are:

- No need to ensure payment is made at correct date.
- No risk for penalty interest.

The technical solutions and contractual obligations connected to direct debit will vary from country to country. Before starting to utilise direct debit you should ensure you have considered the end-to-end process involving the generation of direct debit instructions in your accounts receivable ledger and the proper reconciliation of incoming payments. Furthermore, consider what category of customers you are invoicing. If your customers are not likely to have sufficient funds in their bank accounts at the time of the debit, direct debit should generally be avoided, as any rejected debits usually cause considerable administrative costs.

In certain countries, for example Italy, direct debits are the predominant method of payment for many companies. In some countries, for example Sweden, direct debit is primarily used for consumer payments. In a number of European countries, this payment method is not yet standard practise.

Advance payment

Advance payment should always be sought whenever possible. This is particularly important with large transactions, special orders and orders executed to the particular demands of a customer, where capital is employed to produce something which can only be sold to the ordering company. Each company should have clear instructions for their sales force for when to negotiate advance payment.

Invoicing in advance of services rendered

When selling products which are installed at a client location, or for example consulting services, advance invoicing is an option to reduce the average credit time. An example would be to split the total payment into three parts:

- 1/3 at the time of placing the order
- 1/3 at the time of delivery of the goods
- 1/3 when the installation is completed and inspected.

Of course, this type of invoicing is only interesting if the purchase is of a certain size.

Penalty interest

It is important to state, as early as at the proposal stage, what will be the consequences if payment is not made on the due date. A penalty interest should be sufficiently high to discourage the customer from late payment. Penalty interest is regulated by law in most jurisdictions.

Country practise varies considerably in Europe. In Northern Europe, penalty interest is widely accepted and generally charged and paid at late payment. In Southern Europe, penalty interest is still not considered to be the way in which business partners should communicate, even if one party ignores to pay his bills on time. Cash management is important, but, naturally, the business relationship is even more important and you need to consider local practise and the consequences of utilising penalty interest with some care. However, do not miss the opportunity to utilise this efficient method for improving the payment moral of your customers in those countries where penalty interest is generally accepted. When utilising penalty interest, the interest condition should be stated consistently in every document: the proposal, order confirmation, invoice and the possible reminder letters.

> **Cash management is important, but the business relationship is more important**

Reminder fee

A reminder fee is intended to cover the administrative cost related to managing the dunning process. Reminder fees are regulated by law in some countries. As with penalty interest, country practise varies and you may want to vary your process in different countries. If you decide to charge reminder fees, you should state this in the proposal, as the fee may not otherwise be legal.

Note: The administrative cost for producing and distributing a reminder letter is estimated to 10–20 Euros.

Credit control

Credit control should be performed for each business agreement of any economic importance whenever a credit is granted to a customer. Each company should have a credit policy stipulating, for example, limits for when credit authorisation control must be performed. Often, it is beneficial to purchase credit control services from a local agency.

If the credit control gives a negative result and you still desire to go ahead with the business, some kind of collateral should preferably be demanded, such as prepayment.

Credit control should not be limited to new customers. Procedures must also be in place for continuous monitoring of existing customers. This is simplified if individual credit limits are introduced. The credit control procedures should include standards for holding delivery of goods or services to customers who are late with payments or surpassed their credit limit. Late payments can be an indication that an insolvency situation is approaching.

> **Late payments can be an indication that an insolvency situation is approaching**

But credit control is not always so easy

In reality, it can be rather difficult to apply strict credit control. First of all, the information you receive from credit rating agencies is based on historical information. If the credit worthiness of a company is rapidly declining, you are not likely to receive that information from the credit rating agency.

The second major problem is sales to newly created companies. It will normally not be possible to perform any cost efficient, relevant credit control of newly established companies. "Well", you may respond, "just demand cash on delivery." Theoretically, that is a good idea, and often that is done, but if these companies are part of your target group, you may need to accept that this is a group of companies for which the credit time may be very important as a means of financing and part of what you are selling is then the acceptance of credit risk. If you are not willing to assume that risk, you may choose to buy credit risk insurance.

ORDER

Each day of the order process means that capital is employed. A piece of merchandise which stays one extra day in production or in a warehouse, or a service which is performed one day later, means one day of delay to the receipt of the customer payment. Of course, rapid and correct order management does not only release capital but also increases customer satisfaction and supports increased sales!

> **Rapid and correct order management releases capital and also increases customer satisfaction and supports increased sales!**

Control

The order should be carefully compared to the proposal to ensure the conditions specified by the customer are consistent with the proposal. If the order significantly differs from the proposal in a way that cannot be accepted, the customer should be contacted. If the seller fails to contact the customer, his silence may be legally interpreted as acceptance of the order.

Communication

As soon as an order arrives, information must be forwarded as rapidly as possible to production, stock, distribution, finance and any other department involved. Inefficient procedures for internal communication can delay the delivery and thereby the subsequent invoicing and receipt of the customer payment.

DELIVERY

Incorrect product or service delivery is one of the most common reasons for a customer not paying the invoice on the due date. Frequent errors are delayed delivery, delivery to the wrong address, delivery of the wrong product, delivery of the wrong quantity, unsatisfactory installation or service delivery, damaged goods, etc. Apart from increasing capital employed, poor delivery can seriously affect the customer relationship and future sales.

> **Apart from increasing capital employed, poor delivery can seriously affect the customer relationship and future sales**

Time of delivery

Delivery of products or services should always be performed at the time agreed and according to those conditions which are agreed in order and order confirmation. Any deviation from the agreement can lead to a delayed payment.

Invoicing as per proposal

Sometimes the invoice is delayed because all the information required for the invoice is not available at the time of delivery. In those cases, an alternative may be to invoice as if the delivery had been equal to the proposal. Thereby, the majority of the invoicing will be performed without delay. When all information is available, including any additional orders or services, a final invoice is produced. If you want to use this practise to shorten your actual credit time, state this in the proposal as "additional orders may be separately invoiced". This practise is primarily interesting when the invoiced amounts are very large, as the interest gain must be more important than the cost of producing an additional invoice.

INVOICE

The invoice is not a contract. However, it should contain a repetition of the conditions agreed through the proposal and the order confirmation.

The design of the invoice will have significant impact on your ability to rapidly receive customer payments. Unclear or incomplete payment instructions can lead to the payment being sent to the wrong bank or with the wrong payment method, with a loss of interest as a result. Below, on page 34, you will find a suggestion of how to structure an invoice.

The invoicing activity must always be given a high priority and extra resources should be allocated at peak workloads or when a staff member is absent. Always keep a number of trained backups to allocate to the invoicing function when required.

Increasingly, companies are starting to utilise electronic invoices. Particularly, this is spreading as regards long standing customer relations. EDI as well as internet solutions are utilised. This is a very efficient way to produce invoices for the company which is prepared to take on the investment of implementation.

Time of invoice

Invoicing should always be performed on the same day as the shipping of goods and the invoice date should always be equivalent to the delivery date. Invoicing should not be performed prior to delivery, except as regards service agreements or similar arrangements unless a pre-payment has been specifically agreed. In those cases, invoicing should be performed as early as possible within the contract period, preferably in advance.

Invoicing should be performed on a daily basis. Few, if any, invoicing systems utilised today are so outdated that they motivate any other procedure.

The invoice must also be printed and mailed on the same day as it is created, which should be on the delivery date, as it is important that the invoice reaches the customer as early as possible. Never mail invoices using low priority mail as that will entail delayed distribution.

At installation or service delivery, invoicing should be performed as soon as possible upon the completion of the work. Invoicing on the same day as the completion of the work should, of course, be the goal.

Logotype
P.O. Box 111
111 11 City

INVOICE # :
1234
Date of invoice: 1 January 2000

Customer:
Customer Incorp.
2, Main Street
222 22 Town

Delivery address:
As invoice address

Our reference:
Money Bond
Telephone:
+12-345 6789

Delivery date:
01-01- 2000

Your reference:
Morticia Adams

Your order No.:
22334

Delivery condition:
xxx xxxx

Payment term:
30 days net invoice date

Payment at our accounts at the latest:
31 January 2000

**Payment method
and bank details:**
xxx xxxx

Penalty interest will be charged with x % per year from due date

Invoice design–Example

Content of the invoice

The invoice date should be clearly stated. There must be no unclarity as regards this date, as the due date is frequently counted from the invoice date.

The invoice number should be easy to find as it is often used as a reference and simplifies control for your own company as well as for the customer.

Your own address, telephone number and a time limit for complaints should be stated on the invoice.

The customer name and reference should be easy to find, as well as your own reference and, if applicable, a telephone number to which the customer can turn with queries on the invoice. This information simplifies the invoice control process for your customer and, thereby, reduces the handling time.

The customer order number should be stated in order to simplify the matching with the related order for the customer.

The invoicing as well as the delivery address should be stated, if they are different. It is very important that the invoice is sent to the correct address. If the customer is part of a large corporation, a faulty address can delay payment by several weeks.

The payment terms should always be stated on the invoice and clearly expressed in order to avoid misunderstandings. For example, if you write: "30 days net", the customer may interpret that the payment should be made 30 days from the invoice date, from the arrival of the invoice or from the arrival of the goods. Instead, express the payment term as "30 days from invoice date net".

You may also want to add to that: "Payment should be at our accounts at the latest on xx-xx-20xx".

Payment instructions should specify how you would like the payment to be made, your bank account number (if applicable), etc. The text may be: "Please make payment by electronic transfer to our bank account xxxx xxxx xxxx in the x bank". Payments sent to the wrong bank or with the wrong method will entail unnecessary delays.

If you plan to charge penalty interest at late payment, this should be stated on the invoice, including the percentage rate of the interest.

If you utilise reminder fees when sending out reminder letters, this should also be stated on the invoice. You may want to express that as "If we find ourselves forced to remind you of payment, we will charge you XX Euro against our cost for the reminder letter".

Design of the invoice

The amount of information on the invoice should not be too vast as that will make it more difficult to find the relevant information. Information which is irrelevant to the customer may steal his attention from the important information and cause misunderstandings and delayed payments.

The invoice should be designed to make it easy for the customer to find the necessary information. The information should be structured in a logical and natural way. Therefore, group information which is related, such as due date and penalty interest. It may be helpful to mark the due date with attention attracting colour or frame it.

Credit notes

If a credit note is to be issued, it is usually wise to do this immediately, as the payment of the underlying invoice can otherwise be delayed. Often, the credit note only corresponds to a part of the original invoice.

If you issue significant numbers of credit notes, you should investigate why these are necessary. Such an investigation will often reveal which areas are problematic and how important the problems are.

By measuring the number of credit notes, you obtain an instrument which indicates where you should focus your efforts and where improvements can be achieved. If the level of credit notes surpasses a particular limit, for example 4% of the number of invoices or total amount invoiced, immediate action should be taken.

The number of credit notes, i.e. the number of errors, as well as the procedures for managing credit notes are important for how customers will perceive your company.

The following should be considered regarding credit notes:

- Credit notes should be printed in a colour which deviates from your normal invoices. It should be clearly stated on them that they are credit notes.
- Always refer to the delivery on the credit note.
- Well designed processes for authorisation of credit notes should be in place. Ensure that at least one person entitled to authorise credit notes is always available.
- The payment terms in the proposal as well as the invoice should state that if a discussion arises on any part of the amount invoiced, the remaining part of the invoice should be paid without delay, i.e. on the due date. However, even if you have done that, always send the credit note without delay! The risk of delaying the main payment remains, although it has decreased.

DUE DATE

The optimal situation, of course, is for the payment to coincide with the due date or, even better, to precede the due date (which is more frequent than you may expect, particularly as regards consumer payments). Problems may arise if there is uncertainty regarding which day is the due date.

Correct due date

On the invoice, and all other related documents, the due date should be consistently stated. Expressions such as "available at our accounts" normally means that the customer should initiate the payment prior to the due date to ensure the funds are available on the seller's account on the due date.

RECEIPT OF PAYMENT

Ideally, the selling and buying party should agree together on the most cost efficient method for payment, taking fees, float and administration into account. Usually, a rapid payment method is beneficial to both parties as it reduces the risk for reminder letters and the related damage to the relationship.

Analysis

Payment statistics should be created and analysed. It is important for future negotiations with a customer to know their payment habits — how they pay and when they pay.

If you do not already have such a process in place, it may be a good idea to start by making a list of your 20 largest customers and analyse when they pay, on average, as compared to the due date. Make a similar list of the 20 worst payers. The best solution is if you can extract this information from your information system. If that is not the case, you can pick a random sample of payments for each customer you wish to study and then calculate an average.

Ideally, you should make regular analysis of the average credit time utilised totally and by each customer. It is important that your analysis illustrates given credit time as well as taken credit time.

Credit control

If a customer repeatedly pays after the due date or if a customer shows any signs of insolvency, an investigation should be initiated as to the credit worthiness of the customer. This is an important rule, also as regards long-standing customer relationships.

Customers which repeatedly pay late should be given particular attention and action should be considered, e.g. a shortening of the credit term.

DUNNING ACTIVITIES

The purpose of dunning procedures is to reduce the net amount of outstanding customer debt, by encouraging, demanding and trying to force the customer to pay no later than on the due date.

The goal of your dunning activities should be formulated as a target number of days of average credit time overdue. Ideally, there should not be any credit time overdue at all, but in most industries that would not be a realistic goal. This is an area where significant improvement and savings opportunities can often be found.

Normally, the possibilities to control your accounts receivable largely depend on what has been agreed in the initial proposal and on how well your internal procedures work. Very often, late payments result from unprofessional and inefficient procedures at the selling company. In most businesses, only a small number of late payments result from the customer not being able to pay on time.

Dunning procedures will vary from country to country and from company to company. In certain countries, particularly in northern Europe, it is normal to send a rapid reminder letter as soon as a payment is late. In Southern Europe, a friendly telephone call is sometimes preferred. Below you will find examples of common practice in different European countries. *Note: This is not necessarily the recommended practice, but a guide to understand market expectations and reactions.*

Reminder practices

Austria	2–3 reminders after 15–30 days with 3–4 weeks interval
Belgium	2–3 reminders, 15–20 days interval
Denmark	2 reminders after 2–4 weeks
Finland	Reminder letter, thereafter legal action
France	2 reminder letters, the first one after 15 days
Germany	3 reminders with 2–3 weeks interval, the last one sent from legal counsel
Great Britain	2–3 reminders, 14–30–60 days
Iceland	2 reminders, follow-up by telephone
Italy	2–3 reminders, the last one sent as registered mail
Norway	1–2 reminders, one warning for legal action
Spain	2–3 reminders within 1–2 months
Sweden	2–3 reminders, maximum 60 days, thereafter legal action
Switzerland	1–2 reminders
The Netherlands	2–4 reminders
The United States	2–4 reminders + telephone calls

Source: Intrum Justitia International AB

The sales department should always participate in the dunning activities. For dunning activities to be efficient, close co-operation between the sales department and accounts receivable personnel is necessary. It is important that the sales force recognise that a deal is not closed until the payment has arrived. The sales force must take responsibility for following up on customer payment habits and actively participate in the dunning activities. This is an area where improvements can often be made.

Late payments should be investigated and analysed, so that any inefficiencies in internal procedures can be identified and corrected. It is important to appoint a process owner for the accounts receivable process. This person should be responsible for following up on the development over time and suggest and implement improvements.

Dunning procedures

When the due date of an important invoice is approaching, you may want to take the habit of reminding the customer a few days before the due date. This reminder can be done by telephone, by fax or by letter.

If payment has not arrived within a certain number of days beyond the due date, the customer should be contacted. You need to make a decision on how many days after due date customers are reminded. With efficient procedures, the contact should not be later than one week past the due date and can be initiated by telephone, fax, letter, visit etc. One way to structure your standard procedure may be to start by sending a reminder letter and, thereafter, follow up with a telephone call.

How best to structure your dunning procedures will depend on the nature of your business. At a small number of invoices, the most efficient procedure may be telephone calls exclusively. If the number of invoices is very large, fully automated procedures are more suitable.

Efficient dunning procedures should be performed regularly, preferably daily. If, for example, you send out reminder letters only every two weeks, certain customers will receive their first payment reminder as late as three weeks after the due date.

Reminder letters

The first reminder letter has the following purpose:

- to verify that the customer received the invoice and that he has no objections against it
- to remind that the invoice is due for payment
- to inform the customer of what will be the consequences if he does not pay.

Reminder letters should contain the following information:

- invoice amount
- penalty interest rate
- penalty interest accrued to date
- reminder fee (if previously agreed)
- references to invoice number and order number
- customer reference
- actions which will be taken if payment is not made.

The number of reminder letters should be kept low. We recommend you to avoid sending more than one reminder letter, as the customers will otherwise learn that you will do so, and that they have no reason to pay rapidly.

The last reminder letter, which may be the only one, should state that "no further reminder letters will be dispatched" and that the invoice will need to be sent for legal action unless payment is made. If you threaten a customer with legal action, you must also be prepared to go ahead with such action, otherwise the customers will quickly learn that you are using empty threats!

Make sure that the customer notices your reminders, be they telephone calls or letters. Often a fax will get more attention than a letter, for example, and lead to quicker action than if the reminder is sent by letter.

Case:

We once received a reminder letter which was printed on a paper with a background of a funny little devil. This reminder was immediately noticed, laughed at and passed around the office as the funny item of the day. (That's how much fun we have...) The invoice was immediately paid.

Telephone reminders

Telephone reminders are often the most efficient kind of reminders. If the number of required reminders is large, you may want to establish a limit for the amount of customer credit overdue, and contact all customers which breach that limit, not only by letter, but also by telephone.

Periodically, if you have resources available, you may want to initiate a special reminder campaign, where each customer with invoices overdue is personally contacted by telephone and encouraged to pay his invoice without further delay.

Penalty interest

The main purpose of charging penalty interest is to discourage the customer from late payments, but also to compensate for credit overdue.

Penalty interest should be mentioned in the proposal and stated in all related documents from the proposal to reminder stage.

A penalty interest invoice should contain the following information:

- amount due/amount paid too late
- penalty interest rate
- amount of penalty interest
- number of interest days
- reminder fee (if previously agreed)
- invoice number and order number
- customer reference.

Regular analysis should be performed of which percentage of the penalty interest possible to charge is actually charged to customers and which proportion of the charged interest which is eventually paid by the customers. It should also be analysed why penalty interest has not been charged if this was possible. Frequently, the sales force will discourage the use of penalty interest. Depending on the culture of the country in which you are operating, you may want to challenge the sales force and push for more penalty interest to be charged.

If you are regularly charging penalty interest to your customers, you may want to programme your accounts receivable system not to produce an invoice unless the payment is at least 2 or 3 days overdue. This will save you the cost of unnecessary administration for those invoices which are paid shortly after the due date. However, if you increase the number the of days beyond that number, your cash management aware customers are likely to learn that pattern and systematically pay a number of days late.

Note: If payment has still not arrived 2 or 3 days after the due date, always calculate the penalty interest from the first day overdue, i.e. from the due date.

You may also want to fix a lower limit for when to charge penalty interest, for example 10 Euro. If the penalty interest does not exceed that amount, you may want to keep the amount in your account payable ledger and add it on the subsequent regular invoice.

You may also want to invoice accrued interest even if the payment still has not arrived. This will then function as an additional payment reminder. If you opt for this practise, invoicing of accrued interest should take place at least every two weeks to function as an effective reminder mechanism.

Reminder fee

If you plan to charge fees for reminder letters, it is important that this is agreed at the proposal stage. A reminder fee serves, primarily, to discourage customers from late payments, but also to cover some of your cost for handling the dunning process.

LEGAL ACTION

If, despite your reminder letters, the customer will not pay his debts, it is important to have efficient procedures for taking legal action. This is normally outsourced to third party agents. It is not unusual that consumers, as well as companies, with liquidity problems, do not pay any bills until they are threatened by legal action. Many debtors do, however, pay their debts when this occurs, in order to avoid official records of insolvency.

It is important not to have the mind-set "Why should this case be sent for legal action?". Instead, think "Is there any reason why we should not send this case for legal action?".

Timing

Each company should have a policy for when to take legal action. Each day a case of late payment is not sent for legal action, the receipt of payment is further delayed and the probability of ever getting paid at all decreases. Cases for legal action must be dealt with promptly!

Of course, the policy should also make it possible to choose not to take legal action, but this possibility should only be allowed if there is a valid reason.

Below you will find some examples of normal procedures for taking legal action in different countries.

Legal action/Dunning

Austria	Dunning letter, fax, telephone and visit
Belgium	Dunning letter, telephone call and visit
Denmark	Lawyers monopoly: Legal action must be taken by lawyer
France	Dunning letter, telephone call, specialist bureau
Germany	Dunning letter, telephone call, legal action
Great Britain	Dunning letter, telephone call, 7 days time lag before legal action
Iceland	Letter, telephone and legal action
Italy	Letter by registered mail, telephone call, legal action
Spain	Dunning letter, telephone, 7 days time lag before legal action
Sweden	Dunning letter, legal action
Switzerland	Dunning letter, legal action
The Netherlands	Dunning letter, telephone call, legal action
The United States	Dunning letter, fax, telephone and visit

Source: Intrum Justitia International AB

KEY RATIOS

To be successful in cash management it is important to measure savings and performance. The measurement should be part of the company's regular reporting and not just take place in conjunction with special cash management projects.

It is important that all those who are actively involved in the cash management processes get regular feedback on their performance and accomplishments. This will increase their motivation for continuous improvements and efforts. One type of feedback is the regular measurement of key cash management related ratios.

The same key ratios can also function as guides to where potential savings can be made.

When selecting key ratios, you should consider:

- It must be possible for the unit which is measured to directly impact the chosen key ratios.
- It must be easy to understand and interpret the measures.

One way to use the key ratios may be to challenge different units to compete against each other for the best improvements. This method, in conjunction with classical cash management studies has proved to give excellent results.

Another way to utilise the ratios is benchmarking, within the company or with peers.

Here are a few examples of key ratios frequently used to measure and compare the status of different cash management activities. Naturally, each type of business requires its own type of key ratios. There are no key ratios which apply to all kinds of business.

Examples of key ratios for measuring the inflow of funds

Key ratio	Measured as
Average total credit time, days	Average accounts receivable / Turnover per day
Average granted credit time, days	Average accounts receivable not overdue $\times$ 365 Turnover per year
Average credit time overdue, days	Average accounts receivable overdue / Turnover per day
Hidden credit time, days	Average number of days between delivery and invoicing
Credit notes, %	Credit notes (amount or number of) $\times$ 100 / Invoicing (amount or number of)
Cash discount to customers, amounts	Amount of cash discount, correctly and incorrectly utilised by customers
Payment reminders, %	Payment reminders $\times$ 100 / Number of invoices
Penalty interest, %	Penalty interest billed $\times$ 100 / Average accounts receivable
Penalty interest received, %	Penalty interest received $\times$ 100 / Penalty interest billed

4

THE OUTFLOW OF FUNDS FROM THE CORPORATION

INTRODUCTION

The cash outflow has direct impact on the company's level of short term debt. Just as improvements can usually be made as regards a company's cash inflow processes, improvement opportunities can normally be identified in the funds outflow processes.

The main rule as regards disbursements is that payments should be made at the right time, i.e. on the due date. Paying an invoice prior to the due date increases your capital employed and causes interest cost, or reduced interest income. Payment should not be done after the due date as that may lead to penalty interest, reminder fees, handling reminder letters and, perhaps most importantly, a poor image for your company.

It is also important to ensure that you are using the correct payment method. A well designed payment process contributes to reducing interest as well as administrative costs.

Key points to remember about the disbursement process:

The disbursement process should be efficient and enable control of payments.

Credit should be fully utilised—pay on the due date.

Cash discounts and other discounts should always be utilised as long as they are profitable.

The most efficient payment method should be utilised.

The arrow below illustrates the different steps of the disbursement process. This chapter will describe and discuss the main cash management aspects of each of these steps.

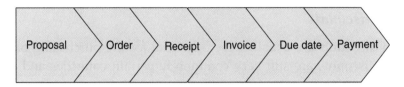

Cash disbursement process

PROPOSAL

The proposal stage is an important part of the purchasing process as this is where the conditions for the payment are agreed. Anything omitted at this stage may affect later stages of the disbursement process.

Always study the small print of the proposal carefully, particularly those conditions which relate to credit terms and payment. If any changes are agreed to the proposal, you should ensure that these changes are confirmed in writing by the selling party.

This section discusses a few areas to consider at this stage.

Credit and payment terms

Your company should develop a policy and guidelines for which payment conditions and credit terms should be sought at different categories of purchases. It is important that these rules are well known by everyone involved in the purchasing process.

Always strive for the longest possible credit terms at a purchasing negotiation, as long as prices and other conditions remain unaffected. Each purchasing officer should adopt the habit of always questioning the proposed credit term and never to accept the initial credit term offered by the supplier.

Naturally, it is important to ensure favourable credit terms are obtained from your largest suppliers. Analyse the credit terms of, for example, your 50 largest suppliers. Thereafter, set specific targets to improve the credit term by, for example, 15 days for half of these suppliers within a year. Very important savings can be realised by improving the credit terms!

Cash discounts

Cash discounts are usually very beneficial for the purchasing party. Cash discounts are still very common in certain countries and certain industries.

Just as the cash discount key could illustrate, above, how expensive cash discounts are for the selling party, the same key can be used to illustrate how profitable it is to utilise a cash discount.

Cash discount key–Annualised interest rate

Cash discount	Days				
	10	15	20	30	45
1%	36	24	18	12	8
1.5%	54	36	27	18	12
2%	72	48	36	24	16
2.5%	90	60	45	30	20

Example:
What is the equivalent annualised interest rate, if the cash discount offered is "15 days −2% cash discount, 30 days from invoice date net"?
The benefit of making the payment 15 days earlier (30–15) is 2%.
Go to the table row 2% and the column 15 days.
Result = 48% interest per year.
Utilising cash discounts is usually very profitable for the purchasing company!

Payment method

You should verify if the selling party has requested any particular payment method and if that payment method is agreeable to you. If the method is not consistent with your preferred payment process, you should contact the selling party and suggest an alternative payment method.

Invoicing fees etc.

It is increasingly common to find you get charged invoicing fees, administration fees etc. In order to avoid these types of fee, you need to pay attention to what is stated in the proposal document. If any such fees are mentioned, you should demand that they be erased from the proposal. Normally, the supplier is not entitled to charge this type of fee unless it is negotiated and agreed in advance of the invoice.

Penalty interest

You should also check which penalty interest rate, if any, is stated in the proposal. If the penalty interest rate is higher than that which is stated by law, you should consider negotiating a reduction of the interest rate.

ORDER

When you, the purchasing party, after careful examination, accept the proposal, the supplier will give you an oral or written order confirmation.

Order confirmation

You should have a standard procedure in place to control that the order confirmation is consistent with the proposal and that only agreed changes or additions have been made.

Invoicing address

If the shipping and the invoicing address are not the same, the person in charge of making the order must inform the supplier of the correct invoicing address. The same person should also ensure that his name appears as a reference on the invoice. Unless this is the case, the accounts payable department may have great difficulty identifying who is responsible for the order, and this will not only cause administrative cost but may also cause a delay in the payment and possibly penalty interest.

Internal information

Internal information is vital to this step of the process. Each concerned department must be informed/have access to information about the order, e.g. production, goods reception etc.

RECEIPT OF GOODS

Delivery is considered to be completed when the purchasing party has access to the goods. The most important aspect to consider here is that delivery is on time, complete and consistent with the order.

Reception control

There must be efficient procedures in place for controlling that each delivery is consistent with the order as regards quantity as well as quality. If any discrepancies are identified, compensation should be demanded without delay.

The timing of the delivery should also be carefully controlled. If delivery is done too early or too late and this leads to any cost for the buyer, some sort of compensation should be requested, i.e. prolonged credit.

Control of the receipt date of the invoice

It is also important to compare the receipt date of the invoice with the delivery date.

If the invoice arrives prior to delivery, this should always be pointed out to the supplier and the credit term should be extended. The main rule is never to accept that the invoice arrives prior to the goods without demanding a prolonged credit term.

If pre-dating of invoices is spotted, this should always be disputed and, also in this case, you should request a prolonged credit term.

It is desirable to agree a credit condition which states that the credit term is, e.g. 30 days from the latter of the receipt of goods or invoice.

Internal information

It is important to have efficient procedures for informing all involved parties, i.e. production, purchasing department etc. that goods have been received.

INVOICE

Upon receipt of an invoice, it is important to have well functioning procedures to handle the invoice.

It should be possible to trace a supplier invoice through the company from arrival to payment. Thereby, you can identify if there are any time lags which can be avoided through more efficient procedures. Time lags can lead to penalty interest, which is a completely unnecessary cost to the company.

Find out how much penalty interest your company paid out last year. Examine the reasons why those invoices were paid too late. Thereafter, you can correct the weak part of the process and reduce the unnecessary cost of penalty interest.

Receipt of the invoice

When the invoice is received, it should be stamped with the arrival date and be registered in your accounts payable ledger.

Rapid registration upon receipt may be important for your ability to reclaim VAT in the right period.

Whenever an invoice is received prior to the delivery of the related goods, and the due date is calculated with the invoice date as a base, the supplier should be notified and the due date be calculated from the delivery date.

Control of invoice

It should be verified that the conditions stated on the invoice are consistent with those specified in preceding documentation. No extra fees, not previously agreed, should be accepted on the invoice. If any such fees are found, these should be barred to make it clear that they have not been accepted for payment.

Cash discount invoices

Cash discount invoices should be given priority to ensure you can pay these on time and benefit from the discount.

Quite often, cash discounts are not utilised because the payment term is considered so short that the company is unable to complete the payment in that time. One simple but successful method to ensure cash discount invoices are given extra attention and avoid ending up in the bottom of somebody's pile of documents is to attach a red sticker stating "cash discount" on each cash discount invoice.

Payment authorisation

The most common reason for invoices being paid late is that invoice authorisation has been made too late for the payment to be completed on time.

It is not uncommon that invoice authorisers handle invoices once a week or even less frequently. If invoices are authorised on a daily basis, late payments and penalty interest can largely be avoided.

One efficient and very simple method is to distribute invoices for authorisation in a red folder (or some other colour likely to get attention and recognition) to ensure the invoices get priority over other mail.

There are also considerably more modern and efficient technologies available for improving the efficiency of the invoice handling processes. Modern workflow technology offers opportunities for rapid imaging of invoices and automated management of the invoice control and approval processes. This is a very interesting opportunity for efficient cash management for corporations which receive large volumes of supplier invoices.

DUE DATE AND PAYMENT

Each company should establish a rule for how to calculate the due date of an invoice. There must never be any doubt of how to calculate the due date and when payment is to be made.

Timing of payment

The target should be always to pay an invoice on the due date. Never earlier!

> **The target should be always to pay an invoice on the due date. Never earlier!**

There are various methods for calculating the due date and the payment date. The most common method is to calculate the number of days according to the credit term, starting on the invoice date. If the due date falls on a Saturday, Sunday or other bank holiday, it is common practice to pay on the subsequent banking day.

Many companies choose to calculate the due date based on the receipt date of the invoice, rather than the invoice date. These companies consider that the credit term is the time the company has been granted for handling the invoice, and thus that it is fair to start counting on the day the invoice is received. Another reason to adopt this practice is that you thereby avoid paying the consequences of any pre-dating of invoices which may have been made by the supplier.

An alternative method, which is relatively common, is to add a specific number of days to the credit term calculated from the invoice date. Companies choosing this method consider that they have a right to compensate for the number of days the invoice was in mail transit. The number of added days should be equivalent to the average number of days the mail would take. Therefore, some companies practise a different number of days for domestic and for foreign mail float.

Analysis

If you want to know when your company actually makes its payments, as compared to the due date, you can analyse a random sample of invoices. Thereby, you can easily identify if invoices are paid prior to the due date (which is more common than you may think) or if payment is made so late that penalty interest is incurred. Pick a random sample of, i.e., 50 supplier invoices and note, for each invoice, the below items. If possible, it is, of course, easier to extract this information from your accounts payable ledger.

Supplier	Delivery date	Invoice date	Invoice amount	Receipt date of invoice	Due date	Payment date	Due date - Payment date	Note
Ernst & Young	05-05-00	05-05-00	500,000	06-05-00	15-05-00	17-05-00	+2	

Analysis of random sample of supplier invoices

From a cash management point of view, it is also interesting to analyse which day of the week payments are made. Usually, a payment which is registered on the suppliers account on a Friday, will not earn interest until the following Monday or later, depending on the value dating practise of the country and the payment method. (This must be examined on a case by case basis.) Therefore, many companies avoid making payments which are registered on a Friday, or other day preceding a bank holiday, as the receiving bank will earn interest over the bank holiday.

If Friday payments are made on Mondays these payments will receive value on the beneficiaries account one day later than if payment had been made on the Friday, but the payer will keep interest bearing funds on their account three extra days. Therefore, avoid making payments which are deducted from your account on a day before a bank holiday, unless you are certain that the beneficiary receives same day value.

> **Avoid making payments which are deducted from your account on the day before a bank holiday, unless you are certain that the beneficiary receives same day value**

Payment method

When choosing a payment method, the method which enables you to keep your funds on an interest bearing account as long as possible should generally be chosen. You also need to consider the fee as well as the administrative cost of the payment method. Most commercial payments will be performed as bulk payments, i.e. paid via ACH clearing systems with one or several float days. (Read more about clearing in chapter 5: *Clearing, payments and receipts.*) These payments are usually the most efficient to process and bank fees are moderate. If you make supplier payments of significant value, these should be paid with same day value[1]. Same day value payments are more expensive to make. The fee is generally higher and, often, the process is less automated. It is easy to calculate limit values for when a same day value should be made.

Example:

Fee for a same day value payment: 1 Euro
Fee for a bulk payment: 0.1 Euro
Float of bulk payment: 2 days
Extra administrative cost, same day value payment: 1 Euro
Interest rate: 4 %

How large must a payment be to profitably be sent with same day value?
That question can be rephrased: At which value X are two days of interest earned more valuable than $1-0.1=0.9$ Euro extra fee and 1 Euro extra administration cost?

$$X \times 2 \text{ days} / 360 \text{ days} \times 4\% = 0.9 \text{ Euro} + 1 \text{ Euro}$$
$$X = 8550 \text{ Euro}$$

This means that, in this example, it is profitable to make same day value payments for all supplier payments larger than approx. 8600 Euro. A similar limit value can be calculated for each major currency used for supplier payments.

Read more about payment methods in chapter 5: *Clearing, payments and receipts.*

---

1 Many companies still choose to make high value payments using corporate cheques. The reason for doing this is that they will then be able to keep interest bearing funds on their account during the time in which the cheque is in the mail. This practise may work in countries where penalty interest is not commonly charged. However, as this is an old fashioned and, in principle, highly ineffective cash management "misbehaviour", we never recommend it. In the long term, you are likely to lose out administratively as well as being penalised by higher supplier prices.

KEY RATIOS

In chapter 3; *The inflow of funds to the corporation*, we discussed the importance of measuring the performance and status of your cash management activities. This is equally important as regards the funds outflow related activities. Here are just a few examples of measures which are frequently utilised.

Examples of key ratios for measuring the outflow of funds

Key ratio	Measured as
Average total credit time, days	Average accounts payable × 365 / Purchase volume per day
Average penalty interest paid	Penalty interest paid × 100 / Average accounts payable

Remember that it is very important that the performance measures actually reach the departments involved. Far too often, key ratios and other statistics are filed in a binder behind the desk of the finance director, for example, without being passed on to the people who can affect the ratios. Avoid that mistake!

5

CLEARING, PAYMENTS AND RECEIPTS

INTRODUCTION

There is a common European currency for the majority of the west European countries, but there is not a single European payment system covering all types of domestic and international payments. The clearing system TARGET, introduced at the same time as the Euro on 1 January 1999, is available mainly for large international financial payments. International payments will still have to be made the traditional way through, for example, the correspondent bank network and domestic payments through the local low value clearing systems.

In this chapter, an overview of the clearing and payment systems available on the markets is presented and explained. Alternative set-ups for domestic and international payments are also highlighted as well as various methods for managing the settlement of inter-company liabilities. We start with an introduction to float and value dating conditions.

FLOAT AND VALUE DATING CONDITIONS

Before describing the clearing systems in detail, the frequently used word "float" will be explained.

The banks charge their customers in three ways, by fees, spread and by float. Float is the time span elapsing when a transaction is transmitted for payment by the payer but not interest bearing on an account of neither the payer nor the final receiver of the funds. During the payment process, the funds are kept by the paying or the receiving bank, bearing interest on their behalf. This is a traditional way for banks to earn money and is a hidden cost for the customer.

A delay of, for example, one day for an amount of 5 000 000 Euro at an interest rate of 5% is a cost for the customer and an earning for the bank of 1 941 Euro.

When calculating the delay of one day, the factor 1.4 is used. The week consists of seven days and the banks are open five days. Taking the weekend into consideration, this means an average float of 1.4 days, i.e. seven days divided by five.

$$5\,000\,000 \text{ Euro} \times 1.4 \text{ days} / 360 \text{ days} \times 5\% = 1\,941 \text{ Euro}$$

Historically, float has not been an issue. It has simply been accepted as a cost in the general bank system. Today, this is a cost factor which is part of the total bank package and is included in the evaluation of a total bank proposal. Most large companies and Groups do not accept the float. They want a transparent pricing of the services provided by the bank. The float, as well as the fee, is a negotiable cost and the trend in many countries is clearly towards a float free payment system.

> **The float, as well as the fee, is a negotiable cost and the trend in many countries is towards a float free payment system**

Theoretically, the move from float to a transparent fee should result in higher fees. In practice, however, cash management fees are continuously reduced because of technical improvements together with economies of scale from handling a large number of payments. This trend is expected to continue.

The payment systems are rapidly developing and at the same time the customers are more aware of the total cost for the bank business. The float must be evaluated as a separate cost in a total bank package. Advantageous value dating conditions and low transaction fees might not be that valuable, if they are combined with high fees for account maintenance, credit limits and poor interest rate conditions. Pricing will be discussed further in chapter 9: *From vision to contract*.

The most frequently used payment standards between banks are the S.W.I.F.T. (Society For Worldwide Interbank Telecommunication) and EDIFACT (Electronic Data Interchange For Administration and Transport) formats. These are standardised formats which facilitate the transfer of the payment information.

The S.W.I.F.T. format is used by banks and financial institutions for international cross border payments and trade finance products. The two payment alternatives S.W.I.F.T. urgent and S.W.I.F.T. standard are marketed to the customers.

S.W.I.F.T. does not only provide a standard for commercial payment orders, but also a standard for inter bank payment orders, messages, credit and debit advises and account statements.

Message types (MT) are classified according to the kind of transaction or message content. There is no message type distinction between "urgent" or "standard", only limited possibilities to indicate the urgency of the payment. It is rather the choice of the clearing route that determines the speed of the transfer.

EDIFACT is a standard format for the exchange of information in electronic format. By using EDIFACT, both internal standard systems and external parties such as suppliers, banks, customs and transport companies can be connected. In other words, this is also not only a payment standard but a format for exchange of information.

The table below lists some of the S.W.I.F.T. and EDIFACT messages commonly used today within the payment area.

Conversion table for EDIFACT and S.W.I.F.T. formats

Type of payment	S.W.I.F.T.	EDIFACT	Comment
Payment order	MT100	PAYEXT/ PAYMUL	Single payments, contains information on transaction as well as details of payment
Request for Transfer	MT101	PAYEXT/ PAYMUL	To make payment orders from accounts in other banks – will result in e.g. an MT100
Payment order	MT102	PAYEXT/ PAYMUL	Multiple payments, which demand an agreement between banks involved.
Payment order	MT103	PAYEXT/ PAYMUL	Single payments , can carry customer to customer info on EDIFACT layout regarding details of payment.
Direct debit	MT104	DIRDEB	Direct debit from the customers' accounts
Multiple Interbank Funds Transfer	MT121	FINPAY	Financial payments
Statement message	MT940	FINSTA	Financial statement
Interim statement	MT942	FINSTA	Financial statement

The banks are using different terminology when explaining the different technical dates in the payment process. In order to have a dialogue with the bank, the terminology has to be clarified and mutually understood. The most frequently used definitions are explained in the table below:

Book date	The book date is the date the client's order is carried out by the bank, i.e. booked in the banks system. This date is also by some banks called the posting, transaction or ledger date.
Value date	The value date is the first/last day on which interest is earned or owed on the transacted amount. This date is also called the settlement or the cleared date.
Clearing	Clearing is the process to actually transfer the amount. The clearing date is the date when the payment actually settles between two banks.

When making a standard S.W.I.F.T.-payment, normally, the transfer is made with a two day forward clearing date, i.e. the payee will be debited on the book date and the remitting bank will earn interest on the total payment amount for two bank days. Depending on the agreement between the final receiver of the payment and his bank, the final value date can be postponed for several days. During this period, the collecting bank is earning interest on the total amount. Furthermore, if the payment is made on a Thursday or Friday, two additional days of interest will be earned by the bank due to the weekend. Illustrated in the picture below is an example of a Thursday payment.

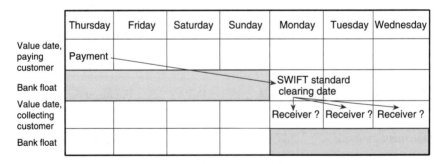

	Thursday	Friday	Saturday	Sunday	Monday	Tuesday	Wednesday
Value date, paying customer	Payment						
Bank float					SWIFT standard clearing date		
Value date, collecting customer					Receiver ?	Receiver ?	Receiver ?
Bank float							

A S.W.I.F.T. standard payment on a Thursday

If, on the other hand, a S.W.I.F.T. urgent payment is made on a Thursday, the transfer is made with a one day forward clearing date and the weekend float will be earned by the collecting bank unless, of course, the payee has a same day value date agreement with its bank. This is illustrated in the picture below.

	Thursday	Friday	Saturday	Sunday	Monday	Tuesday	Wednesday
Value date, paying customer	Payment						
Bank float		SWIFT urgent clearing date					
Value date, collecting customer		Receiver ?			Receiver ?	Receiver ?	Receiver ?
Bank float							

A S.W.I.F.T. urgent payment on a Thursday

CLEARING — INTERNATIONAL PAYMENTS

On 1 January 1999, the change to the new currency, the Euro, and the clearing system TARGET (the Trans-European Automated Real-Time Gross-Settlement Express Transfer System) started. The TARGET system is a real time gross settlement system to which the 15 original participating central banks of the European Union (EU) and the European Central Bank (ECB) are connected. EU countries not converted to the Euro have the possibility to connect to the TARGET system, but at other conditions than for Euro countries.

The following National Central Banks (NCB) and their local Real Time Gross Settlement (RTGS) systems are members of the TARGET system.

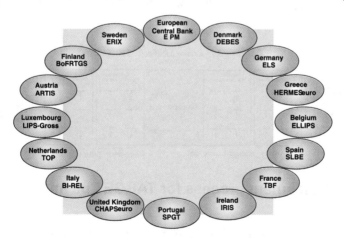

Members of the TARGET system

RTGS systems have during the 90´s been developed by central banks in Europe. These systems were developed in order to reduce the systematic risks that occur in the payment systems. All EU central banks have set up a RTGS payment systems. These systems are interconnected to each other through the inter linking system TARGET.

Target was mainly developed in order for the ECB to facilitate the payment arrangements between ECB and the banks. With this set up, the single monetary policy within EMU could be established and an efficient payment mechanism in Europe was further developed.

The TARGET system is a real time gross settlement system which means that all transactions are settled within a few minutes. Payments are processed item by item and the settlement is immediate and irrevocable, i.e. once sent through the system it cannot be cancelled or changed. By this immediate and final settlement, the systematic payment risk is reduced.

Most banks and payment providers hold an account with the National Central Banks (NCB). The payments are settled through the interlinking systems as illustrated by the picture below. Banks which do not hold an account with NCB can participate indirectly and go through a bank which holds an account at the Central Bank.

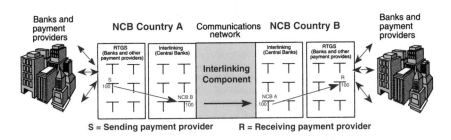

Settlement process for TARGET payments

TARGET is mainly developed and used to settle high value payments. The old methods of settling cross border payments pre

TARGET still exist and will most likely continue to do so also in the foreseeable future. The following settlement methods are the most frequently used:

- Correspondent bank network
- EBA (Euro Banking Association) Euro clearing system
- Group Bank/branch

Correspondent bank network

The settlement of international payments through a correspondent bank network will still exist for Euro payments. It will also be the settlement process for most other international currencies world wide, which do not operate through a TARGET system.

The picture below is describing the settlement process for a USD payment from France to Germany.

1. The customer gives the USD payment instruction to the local bank.
   The payment instruction should contain all relevant information. For a payment in a third party currency, i.e. in this case USD from France to Germany, information about the receiving bank as well as the receiving bank's correspondent bank and the payee's bank account number should be given.
2. The local bank debits the account of the paying customer and forwards the payment to its USD correspondent bank. In Europe, an alternative route is common. Split orders are used, i.e. the payment order is sent directly to the beneficiary bank and a cover payment order (MT 202) is sent to the USD correspondent bank.
3. This USD bank forwards the payment instruction to the correspondent bank of the collecting bank where the local bank is holding a USD account. If both paying and receiving bank share the same correspondent bank, the transfer can be made via a book transfer. If the correspondent banks are separate banks the transfer will be passed through the local clearing.

4. This latter bank then informs the final collecting bank of the incoming payment on the account. When split orders are used, the payment to the customer and the cover order have to be matched.
5. The local collecting bank credits the account of the collecting customer.

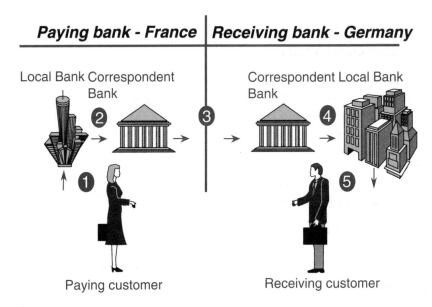

Paying bank - France | Receiving bank - Germany

Local Bank Correspondent Bank

Correspondent Local Bank Bank

Paying customer   Receiving customer

Settlement of a USD payment through a correspondent bank

EBA Euro clearing system (Euro Banking Association)

The large banks active in Europe are members of EBA (the Euro Banking Association). The members are acting in a network as multilateral clearing banks for financial and commercial payments. Once a day, end-of-day settlement, the net outstanding amounts between the participating banks are settled through the TARGET system. Clearing through EBA is not a real time gross settlement system as TARGET, but a net, end of the day, settlement system. The EBA system is also called "Euro 1". The net settlement technique provides advantages in terms of intra-day funding costs for payment orders.

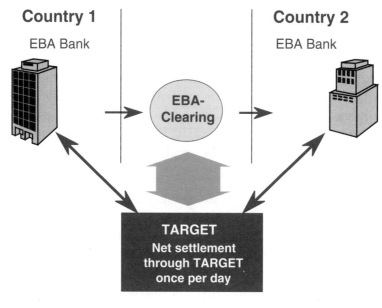

EBA clearing system

Group bank/branch

If a bank has a branch or subsidiary in another Euro country, cross border payments can be settled within the bank. Once the payment has reached the branch or subsidiary, it will be sent into the domestic clearing system or as a bank to bank payment to the payee's bank. The advantage of this concept is that there is no third party bank involved for the cross border payment. Commonly, S.W.I.F.T. is used for communication between branches and subsidiaries, and a similar set of accounts would commonly be held as between correspondent banks. However, few banks have yet centralised their account ledgers.

CLEARING — DOMESTIC PAYMENTS

Almost every country in Europe has developed their own domestic multilateral clearing system. For low value payments, these systems are individually designed.

Basically, there are three different types of domestic clearing systems:

- The RTGS (Real Time Gross Settlement) high value clearing.
- The ACH (Automated Clearing House) low value clearing.
- The clearing of paper based transactions.

When discussing payments, the distinction between commercial and financial payments is made. The majority of domestic payments are non-urgent commercial payments such as vendor and salary payments and are executed via ACH. The financial payments are urgent and usually high value and the local RTGS systems are used for these types of transactions.

The ACH clearing is a local multilateral clearing system to which the banks are connected. In all EMU countries except for Austria, low-value domestic payments are cleared through the local Automated Clearing Houses (ACHs). In Austria, where there is no ACH clearing, bilateral clearing between the banks is used. In each country there are local payment formats. The picture below illustrates the variety of systems existing in the countries connected to the Euro.

Low-value clearing systems in the Euro countries

The low value clearing systems have different clearing cycles, i.e. the time for the payment to be executed varies. For example, the clearing cycle for The Netherlands is two days and for France one day. The clearing cycle will affect the cut-off time for the delivery of the payment information from the customer to the bank. The float is not necessarily affected by the clearing cycle, but float can be taken by both the transmitting and the collecting bank. The float varies between different countries and different payment types. Generally, there is more float for paper based payments (5–7 days is not unusual) than for electronic payments. Some clearing systems, such as the German DTA clearing, are actually funding the system by taking one day float.

PAYMENTS AND RECEIPTS

In this section, different methods for third party as well as inter company payments and receipts will be discussed.

Paper based third party payments

Paper based payments are still common practice in many European countries, although the trend is clearly towards electronic transfers. Examples of paper based payments are traditional cheque payments, Lettre de Change-Releve (LCR) in France, Ricevuta Bancaria (RiBa) in Italy and Recibos in Spain.

There are two different types of traditional cheque payments, the corporate cheque and the bank cheque. When issuing a corporate cheque, the payer is debited when the cheque is collected and cleared by the bank of the payee. When issuing a bank cheque, the payer is debited when the cheque is issued by its bank. A bank cheque is guaranteed by the bank, and a corporate cheque by the payer.

Many European companies are still making a considerable part of their payments by cheque. The cheques are automatically printed and signed by the company and then mailed to the payee. In countries such as Germany and the UK this payment method is still common. Yet, in other countries, such as the Netherlands and the Scandinavian countries, this is rather uncommon.

The border between electronic and paper based payments is not clear. For example, an LCR payment is paper based in the sense that the payee has to sign the individual payment order, but the final payment is essentially an electronic direct debit. In fact, even the signature can be made in electronic form.

Electronic third party payments

Domestic electronic payments

Normally, supplier payments are sent by electronic file transfers directly from the customer's accounts payable ledger to the bank. In order for this transmission of payment information to take place, an interface between the accounts payable ledger and the electronic banking system must be in place. In many cases, individual interfaces between the bank system and the ledger have to be built.

Domestic electronic high value payments are either manually registered in the electronic banking system of the bank or automatically initiated via file transfer from the treasury or ledger system to the bank.

In some countries, for example Austria, Belgium, Finland, France and Germany, there are country specific multi bank systems or formats. With such a system in place, all information transmitted through the system must use the same payment format. Consequently, the same interface can be used for contacts with several banks. This simplifies the change from one bank to another.

Cross border electronic payments

Cross border electronic payments are generally more expensive than domestic payments, and depending on the S.W.I.F.T. message used

(S.W.I.F.T. standard or urgent) there is a float for the paying customer of one or two days for commercial payments. For high value financial payments there is normally no float taken by the bank.

The payment information to the bank is transmitted in the same way as for domestic payments. The bank will recognise the payment instruction as an international payment and execute it as a cross border payment.

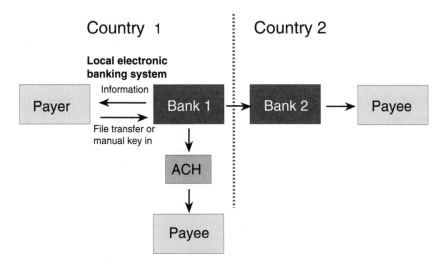

Traditional payment set up, domestic and cross border payments

Local international payments

Companies with a large number of international low value payments are looking for alternatives to the above described cross border payments. One method is to execute the cross border payments as local international payments, i.e. directly from an account abroad into the local ACH clearing system. By making this type of payment, the fee and possibly also the float for the payment will be reduced for the transmitting customer. The fee which the payee is paying to his bank, will probably also be heavily reduced. Thus, this payment method is cost saving for both the payer and the payee.

The client should be aware of the formal legal and tax judicial difference in holding its accounts abroad. Standard practices may also differ as to the information provided through account statement versus debit or credit advises which can affect the matching process. Further, the possibility of controlling payments queued for later payment, or the ability to make queries about transactions posted to the account, through for example an electronic banking system, is vital for this concept.

In order for the bank to offer this type of payment method, it must have a branch in each country or an agreed partnership with local banks. The paying bank has to supply the local bank with the correct payment format or information to be used for the local settlement, for example Bankleitzahl for local German payments.

The most important factor for the bank to consider when selling this method to the customer is to offer a seamless payment process, i.e. the customer should not be affected by the fact that the bank is acting through a branch or an external third party.

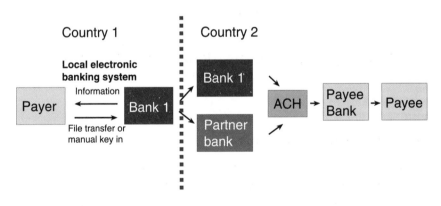

Local international payments

The payment file is sent to the local bank in country 1 and then re-routed to the branch or partner bank where it is finally settled as a local payment through the ACH system. In most cases, the customer has to keep an account with the branch or partner bank in each country to which local international payments should be made.

When evaluating a set up including local international payments, it is important to calculate the actual savings compared to the amount of possible extra administration and costs for additional bank accounts and electronic banking equipment. When there are only a few payments per month, the set up of local international payments will most likely be too expensive after taking the various costs into consideration.

The local international payment concept is under development and offered by a number of banks and will, until there is harmonisation of the clearing systems, continue to be one way forward for companies to make less expensive international payments. The creation of Euro cash pools is expected to accelerate the introduction of international local payments.

> **The local international payment concept is under development and the creation of Euro cash pools is expected to accelerate it further**

Today, many banks are offering to companies transfer of all types of electronic third party payments, i.e. domestic payments, cross border payments and local international payments in one single file, a so called bulk payment*, to the bank. The bank then splits the payments up and routes them, in the correct and most efficient way to the payee.

Paper based third party receipts

When receiving a paper based payment from a customer, the payment has to be taken care of as quickly as possible and presented

---

* See further on pages 78.

to the bank for collection. Every day not collected represents an extra cost for the collecting company.

When receiving paper based payments from abroad, there is a time lag in the mailing system. Depending on which countries are involved, this mail float could be anything from two to ten days. One way of avoiding this international mail float is to use the so called lockbox service offered by some banks. This means that the payment is mailed by the payee to a local address. The bank empties this mailbox on a daily basis and sends the payments by courier to the bank's clearing centre. Credit is then posted to the account of the collecting company with forward value according to clearing cycles per country and the individual value dating agreement.

Yet, other paper based payment methods such as for example Letter of Credits (LCs) and Pagares can be forward dated, i.e. payment will be settled on a predetermined future date.

Paper based receipts are costly in the sense that there is usually a delay (float) before the payment is actually posted to the account, and there is extra administration associated with these types of payments. Preferably, the customers should be contacted and asked to pay electronically. Further, there are more elements of operating risk connected with paper based payments, e.g. theft or loss of the cheque or unidentifiable signatures or amounts. The degree of automatic matching can also be affected by cheque payments.

Electronic third party receipts

Cross border receipts

The easiest way collecting a receivable, but probably the most expensive way for the remitting customer, is to receive an electronic cross border payment to the bank in the home country. The payment will hit the currency account, or if agreed with the bank, be automatically or manually exchanged to local currency by either the bank or the collecting company.

Case: How not to handle foreign currency receipts

In one cash management study, we found a good example of how not to handle foreign receipts. This company had difficulties in handling receipts which were of a different currency than which they had invoiced the client. When such payments were received, they would need to make a manual entry in the accounts receivable ledger. As it was considered complicated to account for the unexpected currency, each payment received in the wrong currency was simply returned to the customer. The customer was then requested to make a new payment in the correct currency. As these payments were often received from foreign countries with less efficient administrative procedures, it could often take 30–90 days to receive the new payment. Furthermore, it was often the same customers who repeatedly made this "mistake". Most likely, these customers had learned that their money would be returned and that they would therefore get a considerable extension of the credit term. Of course, apart from an important float cost, this cash management behaviour also increased our client's credit risk.

The company has now changed this behaviour and cash any cheques received as soon as possible and contact the customer and ask that in the following payment, he pays in the currency invoiced.

Collection accounts

The most customer friendly way to reduce the number of cross border receipt transfers from the customers is to open local collection accounts in the countries where the customers are located. The customers can make their payments as local ACH payments to these accounts.

Cost and administration for the set-up must be evaluated before taking a final decision of collection method. Apart from pure financial considerations, the collection method can in effect be used as a sales argument when marketing goods or services abroad.

Payments and receipts in international Shared Service Centres

With the emergence of Shared Service Centres for financial processes in Europe, new bank products which support international concentration of accounts payable and accounts receivable management in Shared Service Centres, have emerged.

Traditionally, low value commercial payments were only created in the country of payment — otherwise more expensive cross border payments had to be made. In order to support the new Shared Service Centres, a growing number of banks now offer international bulk payments. These are products which allow a company to send one or several payment files to one central point in the bank, containing instructions to make local payments in various countries and with various payment instruments, such as electronic transfers, cheques (which the bank prints and mails), wires etc. The bank will split this file into its components, forward the relevant instructions to each local bank branch and execute the desired payments as local payments debiting local accounts. The customer's file can sometimes also contain instructions for remittance advice to be printed and dispatched. This new product enables the corporation to make all their payment instructions from one central point, rather than having separate financial operations in each country of operation.

Similar files can be created to send direct debit instructions to the bank. One or several files are sent to a central point in the bank which forwards the instructions to the relevant branches for execution of the direct debit instructions according to local standards.

Another key enabling product for Shared Service Centres is the lockbox. The lockbox enables the Shared Service Centre to handle paper based receipts without any physical presence in the local country. Lockboxes can be described as electronic mailboxes. The customer mails cheques and remittance advices to a P.O. box in the local country. The P.O. box is emptied by the bank, which captures the paper based information and transmits it to the Shared Service Centre in electronic format. The Shared Service Centre can then choose to upload the receipt information directly into their accounts receivable ledger or, less efficiently but more common practise, print the information and manually handle the receipt information. Meanwhile, the bank sends the cheques to local clearing for best possible value.

Inter-company payments and receipts

Inter-company invoicing is common in most international corporations. These invoices result in a large number of international transactions in different currencies all over the world. The invoices could be in the currency of either the selling or the purchasing company or in a third party currency such as Euro or US dollars. Most frequently, the invoice will be made out in the currency of the buyer. Thereby, the selling party assumes the currency exposure.

When should netting be introduced?

For corporations with large numbers of inter-company invoices, netting is an efficient way to settle payments. Netting can be used for domestic as well as for international invoices. In general, a company is most likely to benefit from netting if it has diverse product lines, significant flows between international subsidiaries or substantial monthly inter-company FX volume. The feasibility of netting for any given company will depend specifically on a number of key elements, including the number of currencies involved, the number of participants, the number of countries and the volume of transactions. The picture below illustrates a complicated flow of payments in a corporation not utilising netting for inter-company payments. Each invoice initiates a separate payment from the purchasing to the selling company.

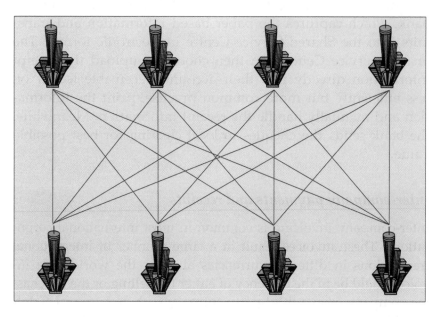

Inter-company cash flow without netting

Performing high volumes of inter-company payments in the external bank system has the following implications for the company:

- Expensive payments
  For each payment, a fee is paid to the bank. Netting reduces the number of external payments, which means that the total bank fees are considerably reduced. Furthermore, if all payments are made in the same bank, the actual fee per payment is likely to be reduced.
- Payment float
  Bank float arises with most commercial payments between

two companies. Using inter-company netting will minimise that float. If all inter-company payments are made as large financial payments within the same bank, it would be normal to perform these as same day value payments, thus completely eliminating the cost for float.

For a company with total yearly inter-company payments amounting to 500 M Euro, one day float represents a cost for the company of:

$$500 \text{ M Euro} \times 1.4 \text{ days} / 360 \text{ days} \times 5\% = 97\,222 \text{ Euro}$$

- Number of foreign exchange transactions
  As each invoice is paid, all entities must make foreign exchange transactions when either paying in or receiving a foreign currency. When netting is used, the number of foreign exchange transactions is limited to a minimum.
- Foreign exchange rates
  When performing many small foreign exchange deals, the currency rates obtained will be unfavourable, as compared to performing a smaller number of large deals.
- Overview of foreign exchange exposure
  It is more difficult to keep an overview of the total foreign exchange exposure of the Group when numerous foreign exchange transactions are taking place in the Group.
- Payment discipline for inter-company payments
  Problems with the settling of internal invoices are common. This creates a lot of unnecessary irritation and is time consuming for the Group.

How does netting work?

Netting is an efficient way to execute and settle inter-company payments. When netting, the number of payments are reduced to one local currency payment or receipt for each netting participant in each netting period. (This assumes that the netting centre performs all necessary currency conversions.)

Netting reduces the number of payments to one local currency payment or receipt per participating entity in each netting period

An internal netting centre receives information about all payments that will be settled in the netting. When setting up the netting system, it is up to the Group to decide if the companies are to report the receivables or the payables to the netting centre. In a receivables driven netting, i.e. the companies which are expecting a payment through the netting report to the netting centre, it is likely that the outstanding inter-company invoices will be settled faster than in a payables driven netting.

The netting centre performs the necessary calculations and announces which entities are paying to, or receiving from, the netting centre. In most cases the netting centre is the finance or treasury department. The netting centre will manage all foreign exchange and will pay or receive funds from each participating entity in the local currency of the participating entity, if it is a convertible currency. In other cases, USD are often used.

Case:

When introducing netting to one large international corporation, the number of internal payments were reduced from 40 000 to 85 transactions per month.

There is more than a pricing advantage to be obtained if all participating entities have accounts in the same bank. This also makes it possible for the netting centre to easily perform all netting payments on behalf of the participating entities, using the EB platform. Of course, proxies from the paying entities will need to be put in place first. The picture below describes the payment flow when netting is used.

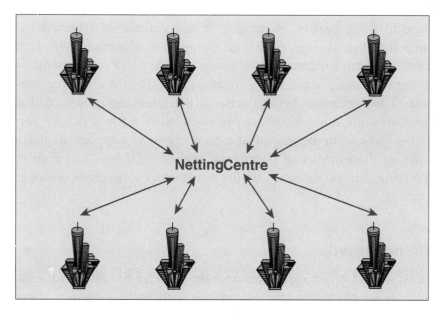

Inter-company cash flow with netting

The reasons for creating a netting centre can be summarised as follows:

- Bank fees, payment float and the number of foreign exchange transactions are reduced.
- Improved foreign exchange rates.
- Netting can be integrated in the total treasury activities, such as foreign exchange management, liquidity management and the management of inter-company loans.
- Improved internal routines for settling of internal invoices.
- Netting is often a first step of centralising treasury. The benefits of netting are so obvious that it will be unlikely that the subsidiaries object to participation. Once the inter-company payment data is centralised, other measures of centralising treasury logically follow.

Third party netting

Netting is primarily used for the settlement of inter-company liabilities. However, it is becoming increasingly common to also include third parties in netting, if the volume of payments is such that the savings outweigh the added administration. In a long-standing business relationship, this type of administrative integration only adds to the mutual benefit of a close partnership. The maximum benefit arises if the relationship is such that the two companies both supply each other with goods or services, but can be beneficial also in a one-way supplier relationship, as the number of payments, and thereby fees and float to the bank, can be reduced, whilst currency risk becomes easier to manage.

The netting cycle

How should a netting centre operate in order to collect information about payments and inform all participating entities about their net assets or liabilities? There must be clear procedures which all participating entities comply with. For example, fixed payment terms must be agreed and invoices must all be paid at a fixed date. An instruction to the participating entities could be designed as follows:

1. Notification	All participating entities send lists of the payments they are planning to make and of the payments they are expecting to receive. (Ideally, this information is sent electronically, but in reality, often by fax.)
	Planned payments and receipts are reconciled. Inconsistencies are resolved by the participating entities, which either access the information electronically, or receive lists from the netting centre.
2. Information	The netting centre performs a preliminary netting calculation with indicative exchange rates and inform the participating entities of their net positions.

	All entities verify the result and compare with their own records.
3. Transaction day	The netting centre sells and purchases currency with 2 days forward value. The netting centre informs the units of their actual positions. The netting centre instructs the bank to perform payments to the receiving entities. The entities with net liabilities instruct their banks to make funds available to the netting centre on the netting settlement day.
4. Settlement day	All assets and liabilities are settled on the accounts of the paying entities, of the receiving entities and of the netting centre.
5. Reconciliation	The netting centre reconciles its accounts to verify that all payments have been made. Any deviations must be corrected immediately, if required with back valuation of payments.

Re-invoicing

Another way of settling the inter-company invoices is to utilise an internal re-invoicing company. The selling company is always invoicing the re-invoicing company, which immediately re-invoices the purchasing company. However, the physical delivery of goods is always made directly to the purchasing company. The selling company is invoicing the re-invoicing company in its local currency and the purchasing company receives an invoice in its local currency. The foreign exchange risk is then concentrated to the re-invoicing company.

The currency rates used by the re-invoicing company must be market based, otherwise there is a risk of a tax penalty from profit transfer between countries. If there is an increase in price through the re-invoicing company, this has to be based on added value for the purchaser. The re-invoicing concept is explained in the picture below.

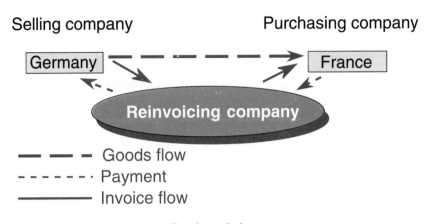

Selling company   Purchasing company

—— — Goods flow
- - - - - - · Payment
———————— Invoice flow

Re-invoicing

Case:

The home furnishing company IKEA started a re-invoicing company, IKEA Handels AG, in 1983. All furniture stores receive a high percentage of their goods from the central warehouses. This creates a number of inter-company invoices in different currencies. By setting up this re-invoicing centre, the payment discipline in the Group became better and the internal reconciliation problems were solved. In addition, the foreign exchange exposure was centralised to the re-invoicing centre and could thereby be managed in a more professional way.

Factoring

Yet another way of settling inter-company invoices is to use the factoring concept. The factoring company could be an internal or an external company.

When using a factoring company, the goods or service selling company is selling the invoice to the factoring company and receives payment for the invoice. The collected amount is reduced by a percentage fee to the factoring company. This fee is dependent on whether the payment risk is transferred to the factoring company or if it stays with the selling company.

The final payment from the purchasing company is made directly to the factoring company. The selling company has informed the purchaser that the invoice has been sold to the factoring company and that the payment should be made directly to the factoring company's account number also stated on the invoice.

The selling company sends two invoices, one to the purchasing company and one to the factoring company. The factoring concept is described in the picture below.

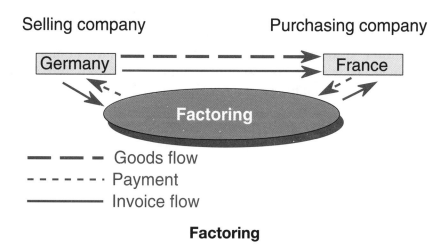

Factoring

SUMMARY AND CONCLUSIONS

Float is a traditional way for banks to charge customers for payment services and is mostly a hidden cost for the customer. Today, more and more companies are aware of this extra cost and do not accept these payment delays. A transparent pricing is the objective and this is also requested by most companies.

International Euro-payments within the Euro zone are still cross border payments. The TARGET system for high value financial payments has reduced the systematic and credit risk for high value payments but these are still cross border payments. The local ACH clearing systems are not harmonised within Europe but act as individual domestic clearing systems for low value payments with different information handling capacity, communication formats and clearing cycles.

Large companies can often benefit from making international local payments, i.e. transforming traditional cross border payments into local international payments through either the ACH clearing or a domestic bank to bank payment. When using this method, domestic instead of international payments are achieved, and fees and float can be reduced for the payer as well as for the payee.

For companies with large numbers of inter company invoices, internal payment systems such as netting, re-invoicing and factoring should be considered. By using these methods, the number of payments as well as cost and float will be reduced. A better overview of the total foreign exchange exposure is also achieved.

6

INTRODUCTION TO CASH POOLING

INTRODUCTION

Historically, all European countries have been working with individual currencies, British Pounds, Dutch Guilders, French Francs, German Marks etc. This is one reason for local traditions regarding different cash management techniques and products, such as domestic cash pooling, domestic and international payment solutions and liquidity and foreign exchange management.

On 1 January 1999, the introduction of EMU (the European Monetary Union) and the Euro, made it possible for multinational corporations to co-ordinate their cash flow in several European countries into one single Euro cash pool. In a first phase, eleven EU-countries joined the EMU: Austria, Belgium, Finland, France, Germany, Ireland, Italy, Luxembourg, The Netherlands, Portugal and Spain.

However, although there is one single currency, within these countries there are still eleven local clearing systems for domestic payments. In addition, a Euro payment from, for example, Germany to France is just as before a cross border payment.

For the four other EU member states not joining EMU on 1 January 1999 (Denmark, Greece, Sweden and The United Kingdom) the existing local currencies remain and will just as before have to be kept in separate individual cash pools for each currency. Pooling of different currencies is possible through the use of currency swaps, i.e. foreign exchange transactions into one currency on a daily basis. Traditionally, this technique was the only way to pool the positive and negative balances in Europe into one net balance for the Group.

This chapter will explain the importance of a carefully prepared bank account structure and analyse different aspects to consider when creating a domestic or international cash pool. Finally, a thorough explanation of the existing different pooling techniques currently available in Europe is presented.

THE IMPORTANCE OF A CAREFULLY PREPARED BANK ACCOUNT STRUCTURE

In the Euro zone all trade will be denominated in one currency; the Euro (€). For companies with business within and outside the Euro zone, it is important to create a carefully prepared bank account structure in order to work as efficiently as possible with liquidity and foreign exchange management, as well as with payments within Europe.

When operating in a number of EMU countries, parallel Euro flows are created. The obvious measure would be to co-ordinate these flows in one common cash pool in order to take advantage of the economies of scale caused by:

- Balance sheet improvement
- Pooling effect — improved liquidity management
- Lower costs in terms of float and fees for payments and foreign exchange

We will now describe how each of these advantages arise. When creating a cash pool, the pooled positive and negative balances will end up in one single currency position in *one* country towards *one* bank. On Group level, the effect will be a reduction of the total balance sheet for the Group, since positive and negative bank balances in most cases will be netted against the bank. The netting will also lead to improved liquidity management, since the spread between positive and negative balances will be eliminated and the net balance can be taken care of in the most efficient way for the total Group.

> **When creating a cash pool, the pooled positive and negative balances will end up in one single currency position in *one* country towards *one* bank**

In the example below, the total interest effect when using single accounts and pooling of balances is illustrated.

Single accounts

	Amount	Interest rate	Interest Amount
Positive balance	+ 80 000 Euro	2%	+ 1 600 Euro
Negative balance	− 50 000 Euro	4%	− 2 000 Euro
Net	+ 30 000 Euro		− 400 Euro

Pooling of balances

	Amount	Interest rate	Interest Amount
Positive balance	+ 80 000 Euro		
Negative balance	− 50 000 Euro		
Net	+ 30 000 Euro	2%	+ 600 Euro

The Euro will be the major currency for many of the large European corporations. Hence, an international cash pool will automatically increase the volumes through the selected bank. Higher volumes imply increased negotiation power towards the bank, which most likely will result in lower costs in terms of float and fees for payments as well as foreign exchange transactions for the total Group. Of course, the total cost saving within the Group when creating an international cash pool is entirely depending on the terms and conditions agreed with the existing banks and the cash flow structure of the individual subsidiaries.

ASPECTS TO CONSIDER WHEN CREATING A CASH POOL

When creating a domestic or international cash pool there are a number of aspects to consider before making the final decision on the pool structure. The correct and perfect choice for one company is not necessarily the right solution for another. Some relevant and important considerations to take into account are discussed below.

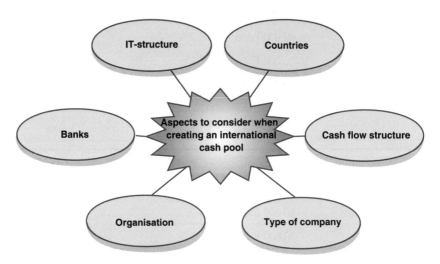

Organisation

Are the subsidiaries within the Group manufacturing companies or are they pure sales companies? If the subsidiaries are manufacturing companies, it is more likely that there will be enough volume and transactions for the creation of an international cash pool. If, on the other hand, the subsidiaries are pure sales companies purchasing most of the products internally, the scenario is not as obvious.

The account structure for the manufacturing company and the sales company will most likely differ. The sales company will presumably have a less complex structure than the manufacturing company when it comes to the need for accounts abroad for making local international payments. The decision how to make internal payments and how foreign exchange transactions should be executed is of importance when creating an international cash pool. Different payment techniques were discussed in chapter 5: *"Clearing, payments and receipts"*.

Banks

What is the strategy for bank relations within the Group? The pooling of funds will increase the Group exposure towards one bank which would create an increased counter party risk for the Group. There are, however, methods to reduce this risk. One solution is to select one bank for the Euro, another bank for the USD and a third bank for the rest of the currencies. Another alternative is to use the selected bank only for cash management related products, and to use other banks for services such as guarantees, long term funding and short term deposits. Yet another alternative is to select different banks in different regions. The solution will primarily depend on the size and financial strength of the company.

Another aspect to consider is whether the selected bank should be one of the company's established relationship banks, or if it should be another bank better suited for international cash pooling. Many companies have strong historic relations with their bank. It is therefore important to take into consideration that the selected bank must be prepared to take quick actions and risks, sometimes at short notice, when there is need for extra short term credits and general commitment.

IT structure

How complex is the existing IT environment within the Group? If the IT structure is not up to date today, the future strategy for development must be taken into account. Are the subsidiaries requesting files for automatic reconciliation from the bank and are they used to very sophisticated electronic banking tools? These are relevant questions which have to be answered in order to create a strategy which will be accepted and successfully implemented by the subsidiaries. Once improved technology is in place, the subsidiaries will start to ask for more advanced solutions. The target should therefore not be the existing level but rather the one of tomorrow.

Countries

Which countries should participate in the cash pool? Are there any legal or tax requirements that must be taken into account when creating an international cash pool? Which countries are, according to volume and general growth, most important for the Group when creating an international cash pool?

These questions should be answered before setting the final cash pool strategy and structure. These answers are also needed before deciding which banks should receive a Request For Proposal (RFP).

Where should an international cash pool be located, in which country? Due to technical restrictions, most banks are only able to place the master account of an international pool in the bank's main location. Tax and legal environments in the country where the master account is set up must be considered by the corporation planning to set up an international cash pool.

Cash flow structure

In order to decide whether an international cash pool is advantageous and profitable for the Group, a business case has to be created. The business case will identify the savings potential for a cash pool. The information needed for this is the average liquidity on the accounts, the existing bank agreements, the cash flow structure in the form of total number of international and domestic payments and the respective volumes. This information should be collected for all individual subsidiaries. The business case will be discussed in greater detail in chapter 9: *From vision to contract.*

Type of company

When creating an international cash pool it is important to consider whether it is a highly decentralised or centralised Group or company.

In a decentralised Group, it might be a problem to have all companies joining an international cash pool where the liquidity is managed by the Group Treasury. If the subsidiaries are measured and evaluated before financial net, it will most likely be easier to join the international cash pool and accept the argument of savings on a Group level.

If an individual country or subsidiary in a decentralised Group already has very low costs and fees with the existing bank and is managing the liquidity in an efficient way, it is not very likely that it will wish to join the international pool. This will create a problem on a Group level, since, for example, a positive balance could be needed from this company in order to increase the total positive balance for the Group and offset negative balances in the pool. When offsetting positive and negative balances, the savings potential is not only the base rate plus a spread for positive balances but also the total spread between positive and negative bank balances. This total spread, the customer spread, is one of the savings potentials in the business case.

In a highly centralised company, the individual subsidiaries and countries will have to act according to instructions from Group Treasury. Most likely, these subsidiaries are measured before financial net. Accordingly, the incentive for active liquidity and cash management is no longer there.

Summary of aspects to consider when creating a cash pool

• Organisation	Type of company — sales company or manufacturing company
• Banks	Counter party risk towards the banks The established relationship bank or a new bank
• IT structure	Current and future IT environment in the Group
• Countries	Countries to participate in the pool Legal and tax requirements
• Cash flow structure	Identify the savings potential
• Type of company	Decentralised or centralised organisation

SEPARATE ACCOUNTS

Separate accounts is simply the option of keeping different accounts in one or several banks without pooling them.

Should a cash pool for the Group be opened or is it enough with individual local cash pools or even individual separate local accounts? There are many questions linked to this subject. Before giving an answer, it is important to know the basics about the different pooling techniques currently available in Europe. In this and the following sections, the different techniques will be presented and explained in further detail.

Why should a company consider opening separate accounts instead of a cash pool? The obvious answer is that there are considerable costs involved in opening up a cash pool. If the company has few or uncomplicated transactions or insignificant balances, the company will most likely — taking the costs for a cash pool into consideration — be better off with separate accounts.

Electronic banking systems can be used to manage separate accounts. The account balances will be presented per account and the company can decide to manually transfer the funds into one specific account. If the accounts are all within one bank, an agreement with the bank for zero float for internal transfers can be achieved. These transfers can be made through the electronic banking system. A manual cash pool where positive and negative bank balances are netted and used efficiently within the company has then been created.

The electronic banking system can also be used for electronic transmissions of third party payments.

The interest rate conditions on separate accounts are generally not that good. But it is, of course, possible, just as it is for cash pools, to negotiate the conditions for the separate accounts even if the average net balance on this type of account is usually not so high.

CASH POOLING — BASIC FACTS

Today, domestic cash pooling is a common product within Europe. There are, however, differences between the various cash pooling techniques offered and used in the individual countries. The three most common cash pooling techniques are zero balance pooling, notional pooling (also known as interest compensation) and single legal account pooling. Before going on to a detailed description of these three pooling techniques, let us discuss a few important aspects which are relevant to all pooling situations.

One reason for the development of different pooling techniques is the different legal regulations within individual countries. Other reasons are the development of the domestic banks' IT-systems and general practice within the countries regarding, for example, interest rates and the degree of competition with other banks.

Only a few years ago, the functionality of the different banks' domestic cash pool systems varied substantially. When selecting a cash pool bank, it was important to evaluate the basic system and electronic banking limitations together with the price. This is still the case for many EU-countries, but in most of these countries, the major domestic banks are offering advanced and quite similar products.

Today, it is not only the functionality *within the individual countries* that must be analysed and taken into account when selecting an international cash pool for the Euro, but also the functionality of a *cross border* international cash pool. Nowadays, three different categories of suppliers for international cash pools can be made. These are:

1. International banks with domestic offices in most EMU-countries, where they act as true local banks.
2. International banks with domestic offices in some EMU-countries, where they act as true local banks.
3. Domestic banks without offices in other EMU-countries.

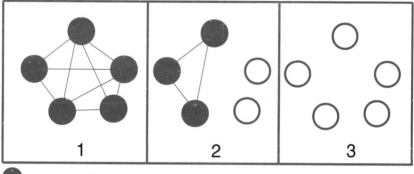

⬤ International bank with offices in different countries

◯ Local banks

Three different categories of suppliers for international cash pools

Tax issues

Cash pooling involves numerous local and cross border transactions. The related tax issues are complex and require proper attention when designing, implementing and operating a cash pool structure.

Even though tax is not harmonised in the Euro zone, the different pooling techniques are not treated that differently from a tax perspective. Three of the issues which need to be considered are withholding tax, stamp duty and services rendered without any fee. These are described below.

Withholding tax

Withholding tax can be levied on interest payments. Whenever the pool master intends to arrange for interest allocation to participating companies in the cash pool, there may be withholding tax on payments/allocations to or from certain countries. This impact is affected by the tax credit capabilities of the pool master, the timing of the interest payment in relation to the tax statements and tax treaties between the countries of the participating companies. The tax rates vary between 0 and 40%.

Stamp duty

Stamp duty is a tax levied on loans received by companies in certain countries. When zero balance pooling is used, inter-company loans will occur on a daily basis between the global pool master and each subsidiary.

Services rendered without any fee

The third tax issue concerns services rendered without any fee. Tax authorities have an inclination to object when they feel that companies are serviced by related Group companies for free. As long as the contributing companies receive compensation for their participation, the tax authorities will probably not object. The cash pool's more favourable interest rate can be seen as a compensation for the participation in the pool.

Internal payments

One of the great advantages of setting up a local or international cash pool is that inter company payments within the Group can easily be made and without loss of value dates. An internal payment within the cash pool will not affect the net balance of the pool.

Credit limits and overdraft rates

Most companies have the objective to maintain the daily balance in the cash pool as close to zero as possible. This is sometimes hard to achieve and negative balances might from time to time be the result. To avoid this problem, a credit limit is usually agreed upon in order to avoid expensive overdraft rates.

One alternative to a credit limit might be to decide upon a positive target balance for the pool instead of trying to balance around zero.

When fixing the internal credit and overdraft rates, staggered interest rates are sometimes used towards the subsidiaries. In combination with the possibility to make inter-company loans and deposits at favourable rates, this will work as an incentive for the subsidiaries to produce accurate liquidity reports and to take the consequences of late payments and subsequent overdraft cost into consideration.

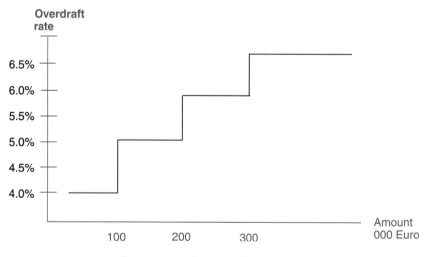

Staggered overdraft rates

Interest rate margins

The interest rate for the total balance of the pool is decided in the contract with the bank. The interest rate is normally based upon an official interest base rate published by the bank. In addition to this, individual customer margins are agreed upon. The interest base used by the individual banks are sometimes individually set by the bank. The customer margin is agreed upon taking into account factors such as the bank's credit rating of the customer and the total relation and business with the customer. The difference between the base rate for credit and debit balances is the bank spread. The customer spread is the total profit of the bank, i.e. the bank spread and the customer margin.

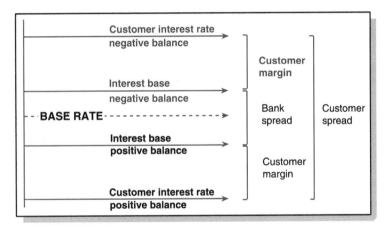

Interest rate margins

ZERO BALANCE POOLING

Basic functionality

All bank accounts in a zero balance cash pool are physical accounts owned by the individual entities with the bank as counterpart. In a zero balance cash pool, all balances are physically swept to/funded from the master account every night. Since all funds are concentrated to the master account, a pooling effect will be achieved. The sweeps can be offered at flexible intervals or at certain balance levels. It is also possible to do the sweep and leave a small balance at the sub account, so called target balances. The daily sweeps will generate inter-company loans, which will have to be documented in order for the subsidiaries to either receive or pay interest from/to the master account.

The bank can also, on a daily basis, transfer the exact amount of the sweep the day before back to/from the sub accounts, i.e. the sweep of the day before is reversed. By doing this, it is easier for the subsidiaries to keep track of the inter-company loans generated in the pool. On the other hand, more transfers are generated.

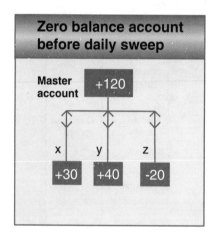 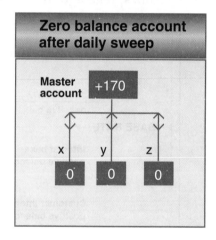

Zero balance account, before and after the daily sweep

The master account is normally managed and owned by Group Treasury. Since all funds are swept to this account, the total interest for all entities participating in the pool will be paid to/from this master account.

Zero balancing is generally an end of day process and the master account holder will need to make funding and investment decisions prior to close of business. Thus, an internal liquidity reporting system will have to be set up for the Group if the maximum effect of the pooling is to be achieved.

Inter company loans

Zero balance pooling will create inter-company loans between the participating companies. Some banks provide a software tool that can track these internal balances and help the pool master calculate the internal interest on the subsidiaries' balances. The interest rate used is decided by the pool master. Generally, this is Group Treasury. The internal interest administration and the tracking of the aggregated value of the sweeps are referred to as "shadow administration". The shadow administration is also used for the reconciliation of internal assets/liabilities. The shadow balances must be booked as inter-company assets/liabilities between the global pool master and the relevant subsidiary. The information compiled within the shadow administration will have to be distributed to the pool participating companies. Most banks expect the customer to be responsible for the distribution of information, as well as for the calculation and booking of the internal interest in the zero balance pool.

Credit limits

Intra day credit limit facilities for the pool master and the local entities must be established to facilitate intra-day payment flows. The intra day credit limit facilities will cover deficits on the accounts during the day and limit the total credit risk.

Normal practice is to structure and agree on price and size of credit facilities at parent company level. A parent company guarantee is also sometimes requested by the bank. Such a guarantee streamlines the process and reduces the requirement for financial information on local subsidiary level. This means that local managers are left to manage the business and eliminates the need to structure credit requirements by each individual legal entity.

Central bank reporting

In most countries, domestic sweeps between residents and non-residents must be reported. This is also the case for cross border sweeps from resident and often also non resident accounts to accounts abroad. Most countries have a fixed minimum amount when central bank reporting is necessary. In certain countries "per transaction" reporting is required, whereas other central banks demand aggregate reporting per currency and purpose. Automatic central bank reporting performed by the bank is a helpful tool for these reports. This reporting tool is not offered by all banks.

Legal issues

The company laws of the individual European countries determine how the liquid assets of a company shall be handled. This has an impact on the zero-balance pool since one of the characteristics of the zero balance pool is the daily co-mingling of funds when all subsidiaries' accounts are swept to/funded from the master account. One consequence from a legal standpoint is that these daily loans/deposits should be documented. The Board of Directors in each participating company will also have to be informed of and accept the delegation of the liquidity management in their company to the pool master. This is also a standard procedure in the handling of inter-company loans/deposits.

Another aspect of the national legislations are thin capitalisation rules that should be mapped out when planning to implement a zero balance pool. In some countries, the thin capitalisation rules set up restrictions regarding the size of inter-company loans, which have an impact on the loans created by the sweeps.

Legal aspects have to be studied in detail for each individual country and group

Advantages and disadvantages of zero balance technique

Below, advantages and disadvantages of using the zero balance technique are summarised. These are facts that must be analysed and taken into consideration when selecting cash pool technique.

Advantages

- All bank accounts are legal accounts owned by the individual entities.
- Control of the total liquidity of the Group is achieved.

Disadvantages

- Shadow administration has to be managed for all accounts in the pool.
- Additional administration due to daily bookings by the entities and the master account holder of the sweeps between the accounts.
- Legally, co-mingling of funds arises and the individual company laws have to be taken into consideration.

NOTIONAL POOLING (INTEREST COMPENSATION)

Basic functionality

All bank accounts in a notional pool are physical accounts owned by the individual entities with the bank as counterpart. When notional pooling is used, the balances physically stay in the individual accounts, but the bank calculates the interest as if all balances were concentrated to one account. In the example below, the balances of company X, Y, and Z stay on the accounts and the bank is paying interest on the net amount of 170 for the pool. Since all balances stay on the individual accounts, no inter-company loans are generated.

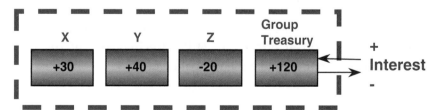

Balance for external interest calculation: +170

Notional pooling

The pool is normally managed by Group Treasury. The interest condition agreed with the bank will be used to calculate the interest on the total net balance. The interest finally received or paid on the net balance will be settled towards the account of the pool master.

Most banks will calculate and allocate interest to each of the X, Y, Z and Group Treasury accounts according to the interest conditions set up by the pool master. The interest calculation on the net position (170 in this example) will take place in accordance with the conditions agreed upon in the agreement between the pool master and the bank and settled against the Group Treasury account. In the notional pool, no co-mingling of funds occurs.

Inter company loans

Since all accounts are physical accounts and the balances stay on the accounts, no inter-company loans are created. Internal assets/liabilities will only arise if the subsidiaries make formal deposits/loans with other Group companies.

Credit limits

In a notional pool, credit facilities have to be set-up for all accounts in the pool, or a limit for the total pool. In order for Group Treasury to be able to invest the total positive balance of the pool, its credit limit has to cover the net balances of the subsidiaries participating in the pool. In the example above this would mean a limit of 50.

If the credit limit does not cover the entire pool balance, the desired pooling offset effect will still be achieved, but the pool master will be unable to use the net balance.

Central bank reporting

Central bank reporting is minimised through notional pooling since there are no sweeps in this set-up. However, international transfers to/from an account in the notional pool must, of course, be reported as always. Cross border sweeps or payments from resident and non resident accounts have to be reported according to the law in each individual country.

Legal issues

The main legal concern arising from notional pooling is the question of balance sheet enlargement for the bank and the Group. Normally, the banks demand cross indemnity agreements between all the participants in the pool in order to be able to net positive and negative balances in its own balance sheet. A cross indemnity is constructed to protect the bank from all damages that may arise from the activities the two primary parties engage in. As a consequence of the cross indemnity arrangement, the bank has the right to present pooled balances net on their balance sheet. Auditors have also, in some cases when cross indemnities have been used, accepted that corporations present the total net position of the notional pool on their consolidated balance sheet. Accordingly, the balance sheet enlargement which traditionally has been associated with notional pooling can be avoided. Likewise, the banks will not have to bear any disadvantage from minimum reserve requirements which formerly made notional pooling expensive in some countries, since only the net position of the pool will be presented on their balance sheet. Through this kind of set-up, the availability of the total net position of the pool to the master account holder is simplified. However, the legal aspects have to be analysed in detail for all participating companies and banks.

> **Legal aspects have to be analysed in detail for all participating companies and banks**

Advantages and disadvantages of the notional pooling technique

Below, advantages and disadvantages of using the notional pooling technique are summarised. These are facts that have to be analysed and taken into consideration when selecting cash pool technique.

Advantages

- All bank accounts are legal accounts owned by the individual entities.

- Control of the total liquidity of the Group is achieved.

- No additional administration due to inter-company loans and shadow administration.

Disadvantages

- Risk for balance sheet enlargement for the company and the bank.

- Not allowed in certain countries.

- In some countries, more expensive due to legislation.

SINGLE LEGAL ACCOUNT POOLING

Basic functionality

Single legal account cash pools are mainly offered by the Nordic banks and their foreign branches. Legally, only one single account with the bank exists, i.e. the main account. To this account, a number of division accounts and/or sub accounts can be connected. A division account constitutes a level to which several sub accounts can be connected. The main, division and sub accounts together compose the single legal account cash pool. However, from a legal point of view, the division and sub accounts can be considered merely an administrative service offered by the bank, rather than actual bank accounts.

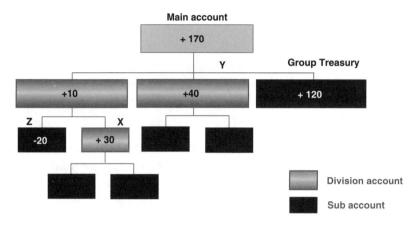

Single legal account cash pool — before action

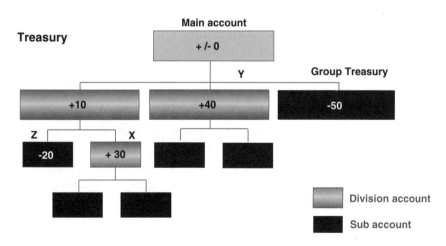

Single legal account cash pool — after action, i.e. investment of 170 by Group Treasury

When funds are received at or paid out from a sub account, the total available balance for the division and main account is instantly adjusted. All funds in the pool are legal balances on the main account. The subsidiaries using the division and sub accounts create inter-company loans to the main account and do not legally have any assets or liabilities towards the bank. The main account is normally managed and owned by Group Treasury.

All division and sub account holders receive individual bank account numbers and the individual balances are presented per account by the bank. A subsidiary can work exactly in the same way as if the account had been a separate account and not connected to any pool.

No transactions can take place on the main and division accounts. These accounts only work as summary accounts. The total balance in the pool can be viewed on the main account, but the total pool balance must be managed through a sub account.

The interest condition agreed upon with the bank will be applied to the balance of the main account. The main account holder will set the individual interest rates on the sub accounts. The Nordic banks supply the main account holder with shadow administration and interest capitalisation on sub accounts.

Inter-company loans

All balances on division and sub accounts generate inter-company loans towards the main account holder, and the balances should be booked as an internal asset or liability. The administration of the loans will be taken care of by a shadow administration system offered by most banks.

Credit limits

A credit limit can be established for the main account. Price and size of credit facilities are agreed with the main account holder. Credit limits can also be allocated to the individual sub accounts. However, since the only legal account with the bank is the main account, the bank will generally not take any legal responsibility for any internal misuse of the credit limits within the pool, i.e. the pool master will have to monitor if the holders of the sub accounts create overdrafts on their accounts.

Central bank reporting

Domestic central bank reporting is minimised also with the single legal account pooling method, since all payments will legally hit the account of the pool master. Cross border sweeps or payments will have to be reported according to the law in each individual country.

Legal issues

Earlier comments for zero balance pooling are also valid for single legal account pooling. The company laws of the individual European countries restrict the co-mingling of funds. The pool master must **at all times** be updated on the subsidiaries´ capability of repaying the outstanding loans. If this is not the case, the loan could be looked upon as an indirect dividend.

The bank offering the total credit limit for the pool has to offer control of the individually set credit limits as well as the total credit limit of the pool. This is, however, not the actual capability of most banks.

Advantages and disadvantages of single legal account pooling

Below, advantages and disadvantages of using the single legal account pooling technique are summarised. These are facts that have to be analysed and taken into consideration when selecting cash pool technique.

Advantages

- Control of total liquidity for the Group is achieved.
- Limited administration.

Disadvantages

- Not all accounts are legal accounts with the bank, owned by the subsidiaries.

- Legally, co-mingling of funds is created.

- Sold and marketed mainly by Nordic banks.

MULTI CURRENCY POOLING

What about pooling including different currencies? Multi currency pooling is a product offered by many banks. Daily, the bank makes a spot and a forward foreign exchange transaction (a swap) between the actual currencies and the selected base currency for the pool. A pooling effect for the different currencies is achieved. Interest is paid on the total balance.

The objective of pooling the liquidity for the Group is achieved. The disadvantage is that the overview of the cost for the pool is lost since the cost for the swaps is virtually impossible to follow up. Therefore, most companies choose to make the swaps on their own. This product is best suited for somewhat smaller Groups that cannot obtain economies of scale by having active liquidity management performed by Group Treasury.

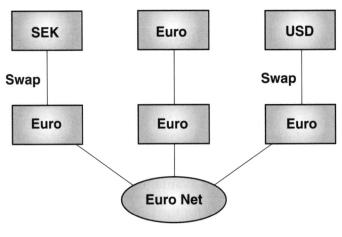

Multi currency pooling

SUMMARY

When setting up a new cash pool structure for a Group it is important to analyse all different aspects relevant for the Group to consider before finalising the vision. Once the vision is set and presented to banks and subsidiaries it is much more difficult to make changes and adjustments.

Below, a summary of the effect of the different pooling techniques presented in this chapter, i.e. zero balance, notional and single legal account pooling, is presented.

Effect of different pooling techniques

	Zero balance pooling	Notional pooling	Single legal account pooling
Pooling effect achieved	YES	YES	YES
Each accounts legal account with the bank	YES	YES	NO
Creation of inter-company loans	YES	NO	YES
Additional administration	YES	NO	NO
Balance sheet enlargement for the bank	NO	IN SOME COUNTRIES	NO
Balance sheet enlargement for the Group	NO	IN SOME COUNTRIES	NO

- Pooling effect achieved
  All techniques achieve the objective of pooling the total available balances and liquidity for the Group. The difference is how the pooling is achieved, i.e. through physical or notional pooling.
- Each accounts legal account with the bank
  This is not true for the single legal account pooling technique. With this technique, there is only one legal account with the bank. All other accounts are administrative accounts with dedicated internal bank account numbers.

- Creation of inter company loans
  Inter-company loans are created in the zero balance and single legal account pooling technique. In a notional pool, however, all balances physically stay on the accounts. Consequently, no inter-company loans are created.
- Additional administration
  Inter-company loans create additional administration. Automatic book keeping procedures can be implemented, but do not entirely eliminate some manual extra work.
- Balance sheet enlargement for the bank
  When using zero balance or single legal account pooling methods, there is no risk of balance sheet enlargement for the bank. In a zero balance pool, the positive and negative balances are physically netted, and in the Nordic pools there is only one legal account with the bank. For notional pooling, however, balance sheet enlargement will depend on the legal restrictions in the country where the pooling takes place.
- Balance sheet enlargement for the Group
  For zero balance and single legal account pooling, the same answer applies to the question of balance sheet enlargement for the Group as for balance sheet enlargement for the bank. For notional pooling, the auditors of the Group and bank will have to interpret the legal aspects when consolidating the balance sheet.

7

EFFICIENT INTERNATIONAL BANK ACCOUNT MANAGEMENT

INTRODUCTION

In chapter 6: *Introduction to cash pooling*, the different cash pooling techniques available in Europe were described. In this chapter, different options for using and combining these techniques for efficient international bank account management will be discussed.

When pooling across borders, there are three issues that have to be considered.

1. The choice of pooling per entity or by country.
2. Analysis of the different cross border pooling techniques, i.e. notional, zero balance or single legal account pooling.
3. Selection of bank concept, i.e. single, overlay or local bank.

These three steps will be explained in further detail in this chapter.

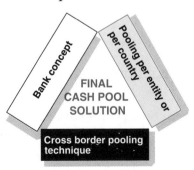

Issues to consider when pooling across borders

NO CO-ORDINATION OF FOREIGN OPERATIONS

Historically, many multinational corporations have chosen not to co-ordinate their foreign treasury management operations in Europe. One reason for this was the number of currencies existing in Europe. As a result of the currency diversity, most European subsidiaries of international Groups are responsible for their own day to day liquidity and cash management. Group head office controls the cash management only through regular reporting received from the subsidiaries.

No co-ordination of foreign operations

Local cash pools per country are sometimes established, but it is not that unusual to find a great number of bank contacts per subsidiary as well as multiple sets of accounts for both local and foreign currencies. The first step towards cross border co-ordination is to co-ordinate within the individual countries. This co-ordination does not necessarily have to take place before the international co-ordination but should be taken into account when implementing a new Group cash pool structure.

Is co-ordination and cross border pooling always the most correct and advisable solution for all companies? The answer is probably no. Regular fund transfers and the set-up of collection accounts, i.e. bank accounts abroad to which foreign customers can make local payments, might be just as good, depending on the cash flow situation and the type of company.

The best way to decide whether to co-ordinate or not is to make a business case in order to identify the savings potential for an international cash pool. The business case is discussed in further detail in chapter 9: *From vision to contract.*

POOLING PER ENTITY OR BY COUNTRY

When planning for an international cross border cash pool, one of the first choices to make is whether to pool per entity or per country.

Pooling per entity

When pooling per entity, all cross border sweeps are made per legal entity. Before such sweeps take place, local pooling per country is made per subsidiary. This will, compared to pooling by country, increase the total number of cross border sweeps for the Group and, consequently, increase the total cost for the Euro cash pool. On the other hand, less administration for inter-company loans is achieved. The subsidiaries will also get a better overview of their available total balance since all balances are concentrated into one account on a daily basis at the end of the day.

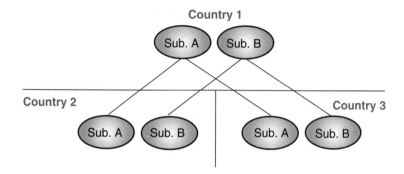

Pooling per entity

Pooling per entity will improve and simplify the payment procedures, netting, inter company loans and foreign exchange transactions since all accounts for all subsidiaries are held in one bank in the same country.

Cross border pooling per entity is more likely to be successful using a single bank concept (see page 130 for further reading).

Pooling per country

When pooling per country, local pooling can be performed per subsidiary or division followed by pooling to a national top account or directly to the national top account. This top account is normally owned and managed by Group Treasury. Finally, cross border pooling is made from the Group Treasury account to the central pool.

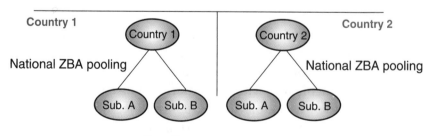

Pooling per country

The total number of accounts in the pool as well as the number of cross border sweeps will be smaller, as compared to pooling per entity, but the number of accounts for Group Treasury will increase since they will be a member of all local cash pools established. Depending on the structure of the company, this alternative will most likely increase the administration due to the large number of accounts and inter-company loans. A well developed internal shadow administrative system can simplify this process.

Pooling per country could be used with any bank concept selected, i.e. single, overlay or local bank.

CROSS BORDER POOLING — ALTERNATIVE POOLING TECHNIQUES

When pooling across borders, different techniques can be combined for national and global pooling. In the table below, six alternatives are outlined. These six alternatives will be analysed in further detail in this chapter.

Alternative international pooling combinations

	Global technique
1. national zero balance pooling	1. zero balance pooling
2. national zero balance pooling	2. notional pooling
3. cross border zero balance pooling per entity	3. zero balance pooling
4. cross border zero balance pooling per entity	4. notional pooling
5. national notional pooling	5. notional pooling
6. national notional pooling	6. zero balance pooling

The above alternatives are conceptual. In reality, a mixture of techniques is normally needed in order to avoid legal and tax restrictions in individual countries. Today, all cross border pooling must be physical. Notional pooling across borders is not a product offered by the banks due to legal restrictions.

The single legal account pooling technique described earlier, in chapter six, is not included in the analysis since the offering of this pooling technique is limited. However, single legal account pooling is similar to and can be compared with zero balance pooling.

National and global zero balance pooling

Using national and global zero balance pooling, all bank accounts in each country are pooled to a national zero balance pool. The zero balance technique is used for both the national pooling and the cross border pooling of the national balances. The top account holder in the national pool and the master account holder in the global pool will most likely be Global Treasury for the Group. On a daily basis, Global Treasury will pool all national balances into the global master account. The concept is illustrated below.

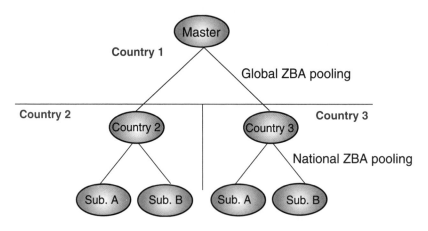

National and global zero balance pooling

National zero balance pooling — global notional pooling

With national zero balance pools combined with a global notional pool, all bank accounts in each country are pooled to a national zero balance pool. The top account holders of the national pools make cross border transfers to their own accounts in the Global pool. The notional pooling technique is used globally. This method is an alternative when different subsidiaries or entities are top account holders in the national pools. The master account holder in the global notional pool will most likely be Global Treasury for the Group. The concept is illustrated below.

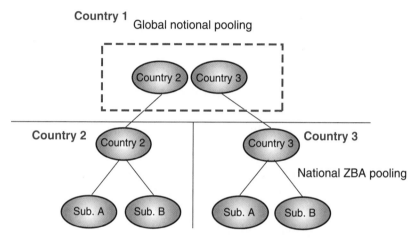

National zero balance pooling — global notional pooling

Cross border zero balance pooling per entity — global zero balance pooling

In a cross border zero balance pool per legal entity, all operating accounts in the various pools are opened in the name of the subsidiary. The balances in these pools are transferred to the country selected for the global pooling from which the final zero balance pooling to the top account will take place. If, however, the entity balance is negative, additional funds will be transferred to the entity from the respective entity account in the global pool. The transfer can, of course, also be made directly from the subsidiaries to the master account, but this would mean increased administration due to a larger number of internal loans. The concept is illustrated below.

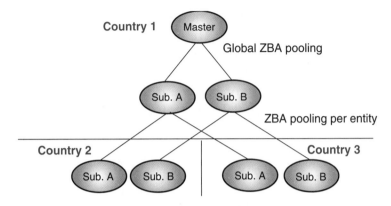

Cross border zero balance pooling per entity — global zero balance pooling

Cross border zero balance pooling per entity — global notional pooling

In a cross border zero balance pool per legal entity, all operating accounts in the various pools are opened in the name of the subsidiary. The balances in these pools are transferred to the country selected for the global pooling from which the final notional pooling will take place. If the country balance is negative, additional funds will be transferred to the country from the respective account in the global pool. The concept is illustrated below.

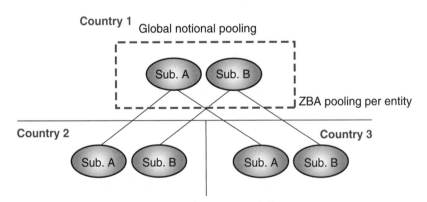

Cross border zero balance pooling per entity — Global notional pooling

National and global notional pooling

In a national and global notional pool, the balances are notionally pooled per country. The master account holders of the national notional pools make cross border transfers to their own accounts in the country selected for the Global pool, where the final global notional pooling will take place. The master account holder of the global notional pool will most likely be Global Treasury for the Group. The concept is illustrated below.

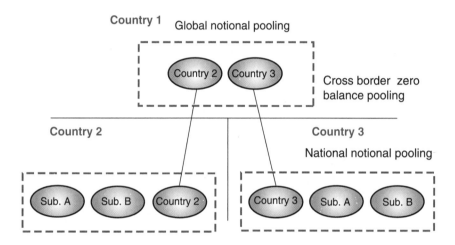

National and global notional pooling

National notional pooling — global zero balance pooling

In a national notional pool combined with a global zero balance pool, the balances are notionally pooled per country. The master account holders of the national notional pools make cross border transfers to the master account holder in the country selected for the Global pool. The master account holder of the global zero balance pool will most likely be Global Treasury for the Group. The concept is illustrated below.

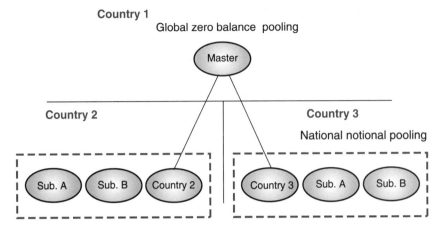

National notional pooling and global zero balance pooling

Summary and conclusions

Summary

Before creating the final vision for a future cross border cash pool, international bank account management should be discussed in detail within the Group. If the concept finally decided for the Group does not fit the individual entities or subsidiaries, it will most likely be very difficult to implement. Therefore, it is worthwhile analysing these alternatives in detail.

Some of the aspects to consider when evaluating the different pooling techniques are listed below.

- Accounting for transfers
  All sweeps in a zero balance pool have to be accounted for. Naturally, this is avoided with notional pooling since there are no sweeps. However, it is possible to arrange automatic booking of transfers for zero balance pooling.
- Inter company loans
  Zero balance pooling creates inter-company loans within the Group. This is avoided with notional pooling. When pooling per entity, the number of inter-company loans decreases.

- Number of cross border sweeps
  Cross border sweeps are more costly than domestic sweeps, especially if the sweeps are made between different banks. A large number of cross border sweeps will generally be required if cash pooling per legal entity is chosen.
- Overview for subsidiaries
  When pooling the balances for all accounts belonging to one subsidiary into one account, it is easy to get an overview of the total balance.
- Need for local cash pool
  When pooling per legal entity, no local cash pool is established. This will reduce the administration.
- Cost
  Pooling per entity will increase the number of cross border sweeps and the total number of accounts in the pool. Consequently, the cost for the total pool will increase.

Conclusion

This evaluation shows that there are a fair number of pros and cons for all alternatives. In practice, different Groups will emphasise and evaluate the criteria differently, depending on size, complexity, general demands and IT-maturity. For one Group the most important factor might be the possibility to get an overview of the balance per subsidiary. For another, cost might be the dominating driver. Thus, there is no general right or wrong when choosing a cash pooling solution.

CROSS BORDER POOLING — ALTERNATIVE BANK CONCEPTS

Earlier in this chapter, the different cross border pooling techniques and pooling per entity and country have been analysed. Still to be dealt with and one of the most strategic decisions in this process, is the selection of bank concept.

The selection of bank concept and bank is very sensitive. In this process, we always recommend that the subsidiaries are involved in both the evaluation and the selection phase. If the subsidiaries must exchange a well established house bank for a new and for them untested foreign bank, management has to ensure buy-in from the subsidiaries.

In the future, companies will most likely use fewer banks than they do today. This does not necessarily mean that a company will use only one bank. The question for companies is what bank concept will best serve them both locally and internationally in Europe when pooling across borders.

When creating the final company specific international cash management vision, it should always be a realistic solution. The bank concept selected has to be available on the market or at least possible to implement within the near future. It must also be an efficient solution for Group Treasury as well as for all involved subsidiaries.

> **The bank concept selected has to be available on the market or at least possible to implement within the near future**

The following three bank concepts for international cross border pooling will be discussed and analysed in this chapter;

- Local cash pool — Multi bank concept
- Overlay structure
- Single bank concept
  - Single cash pool concept
  - Single bank account concept

Local cash pool — Multi bank concept

With a local bank concept, one local cash pool bank per country is chosen. The local cash pool bank can be selected in two different ways. The straight forward approach is to continue working with the banks traditionally used by the subsidiaries. The alternative is to enter a formal selection process where a general request for proposals is sent to the banks considered to be strong in each particular country.

In addition to the local banks, the global pool bank to where the balances from the local cash pools are pooled is selected. From the local banks, regular, for example daily or weekly, manual or automatic transfers are made to/from the global pool bank. Group Treasury then takes care of the balance arising at the global pool bank.

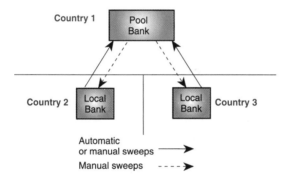

Local cash pool–Multi bank solution

The local cash pool concept is mainly preferred among highly decentralised Groups where most decisions are taken locally. Groups largely depending on strong local bank relations also find this concept attractive.

Daily cross border transfers of the available bank balances are made between the global and the local banks. Depending on the agreements between the selected banks, the level of automatic transfers or so called sweeps vary. Generally, some manual transfers have to be made before the daily total liquidity is available on the global account or the possible deficits are covered on the local accounts.

By selecting different local banks, local payments will most likely be executed from these banks. However, cross border payments may be made from the pool bank. Payment alternatives were discussed in chapter 5: *Clearing, payments and receipts.*

A local cash pool solution will probably be a more expensive solution than a single bank solution, since the volumes per bank are smaller and, hence, the company has a weaker negotiating position. On the other hand, the subsidiaries are able to keep their existing bank partners.

This kind of solution could take somewhat longer to implement, due to the fact that there are a number of interfaces and new systems that must be implemented, set up and connected to the global bank. There are also a number of different banks where mutual understanding should be established.

The partner bank concept

The partner bank concept is under development between banks which are not capable of offering pan European cash management services on their own. Banks which are strong in complementing regions form partnerships in order to be able to serve corporations with international cash management requirements. This is a most important concept for many banks to develop. Without a well established and working network, they will not be able to offer an efficient Euro cash pool solution for their international corporate customers.

After having selected the global cash pool bank, their local partner banks can be used by the Group. Price and general conditions for the partner banks as well as knowledge about the services and systems offered, will be obtained via the global bank. Several banks are in the process of establishing these partnership relations.

Overlay structure

With an overlay structure, a global cash pool bank is selected. As with the local cash pool structure one local bank per country is chosen. The local cash pool bank could be either a partner bank, a local bank or even the global pool bank.

In addition to the local bank, the global cash pool bank will open an overlay account in each country. On a regular basis, the local concentration of funds per country will be made to this account for further transfer to the global pool.

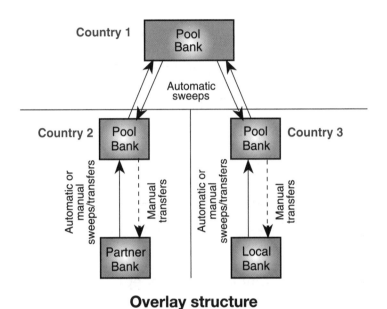

Overlay structure

The advantage of an overlay structure compared to a local bank structure is that the cross border transfers are made within one bank: i.e. the cost for the daily cross border sweeps to and from the global pool to the overlay accounts abroad will be minimised. The sweeps can also be automated, since the transfers are made within one single bank. The risk of loosing value dates, i.e. float, for the cross border transfers is thus reduced.

When opting for an overlay structure there is a good selection of banks to choose between. Even though many banks are not fully adequate local cash management banks, they are represented in the country and can act as overlay bank.

One of the advantages of this solution is the option for the subsidiaries to keep a local bank, which implies that new bank relations do not have to be established. The disadvantage is, however, the cost for the set up due to the number of accounts and banks and the possible increase in time for implementation.

Single bank concept

With a single bank concept, *one* bank is selected as both the global and local cash pool bank. This bank will serve all subsidiaries with domestic as well as international payments.

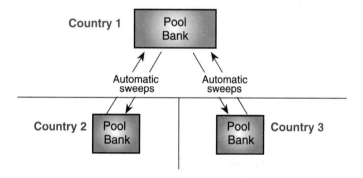

Single bank concept

A single bank solution is clearly the optimal set up from a pooling point of view. However, one of the disadvantages with this solution is the limited number of banks offering this concept. A true single bank concept including all Euro countries does not exist today. A single bank concept can be established, but depending on the countries in which the Group is located, exceptions most likely have to be accepted. In practice, the overlay and local bank solution is often used together with the single bank solution.

For a Group with a shared service centre in place for Treasury and cash management, the single bank concept is a very attractive solution. This especially since Groups with shared service centres often have or are on their way to install a streamlined IT-structure with well developed ERP-systems, i.e. very few interfaces will have to be created between the bank and the Group. With the introduction of a shared service centre, the processes in the individual countries have been standardised, which also makes it attractive to consider the single bank concept.

The counter party risk is heavily increased when the liquidity for the total Group is centralised to one bank during the entire day. One way to reduce this risk is active liquidity management by external bank deposits or purchase of securities. Moreover, the local support from domestic banks will not be there, which some subsidiaries most likely will consider to be a disadvantage.

The advantages of this concept are quite obvious. By using one single bank, a truly automated global cash pool can be implemented and one central negotiation for all countries will take place. Because of the large volumes and number of transactions to be executed from this single bank, the cost of the pool will most likely be less than for a local or an overlay cash pool.

Single cash pool concept

The single cash pool concept is a further development of the single bank concept. In this solution, only one cash pool for all subsidiaries in the Group is established in one country. From this account all domestic and international payments for all subsidiaries in the Group are executed.

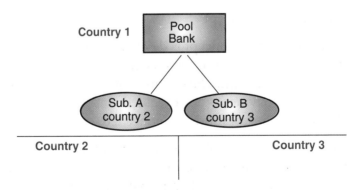

Single cash pool concept

The domestic clearing systems currently in place in the Euro zone are all individual systems without any integration. In order to make local payments, these have to be executed via local accounts. With a single cash pool concept, the bank has to be able to provide international domestic payments through accounts belonging to the bank. Otherwise, all international payments will be cross border payments. This will be a very expensive solution for Groups with a lot of international payments.

Most likely, in addition to the single cash pool, local accounts with small balances will be kept by the subsidiaries for salaries and petty cash.

In addition, customers outside the country where the cash pool is located will have to make cross border payments, which for them is expensive. This set-up is therefore to be recommended only to companies with limited export or where foreign receipts are large and infrequent. If this is not the case, local collection accounts ought to be set-up, i.e. accounts to where the customers can make domestic payments. These accounts will then, on a regular basis, be swept to the single cash pool.

Once the development of the clearing systems within the Euro zone are harmonised, this will be the obvious solution for the future.

Single bank account concept

The single bank account concept is developed from the single cash pool concept. In this solution, there is only one bank account per currency for the total Group. From this single account all domestic and international payments are executed. In other words, additional physical pooling of funds is not needed.

This solution is only possible to implement if the Group has enough in house administrative capabilities to efficiently allocate internal and external payments and receipts to the correct subsidiaries within the Group.

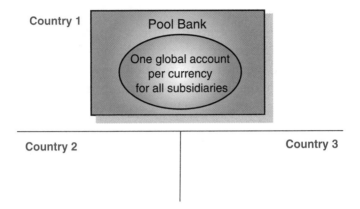

Single bank account concept

Summary and conclusions

Summary

Which concept should be selected? The question is difficult to answer and there is never an answer which is truly right or wrong. Each Group will have to make a decision based on the individual circumstances of the Group.

The table below is a summary and analysis of general aspects to consider when selecting the bank concept.

	Local bank concept	Overlay concept	Single bank concept
Negotiation power	−	−	+
Pooling effects & liquidity management	+	+	+
Number of bank relations	−	−	+
New bank relations for subsidiaries	+	+	−
Cost	−	+/−	+
Counter party exposure	+	+	−
Manual sweeps	−	−	+
Number of accounts	+	−	+
Local banking capabilities	+	+	−

- Negotiation power
  Clearly, when concentrating the cash management requirements for a total Group to one bank the negotiation power
  increases, and increased negotiation power leads to better
  prices. Cash management systems are expensive for the
  banks to develop and maintain. Large volumes are therefore
  needed.
- Pooling effects and liquidity management
  All three concepts fulfil the objective of pooling the liquidity
  for the Group. A distinction between the concepts can be made
  when comparing the amount of manual efforts in order to
  achieve the objective. Automatic sweeping functions for local
  and global pooling is preferred.
- Number of bank relations
  A large number of bank relations could be interpreted as both
  positive and negative within a Group. Group Treasury on the
  other hand most likely prefer the single bank solution because
  of practical reasons, such as the limited number of contracts
  that have to be negotiated and the simplified electronic banking set-up and maintenance. When selecting the single bank
  concept, it is of utmost importance for the Group to make sure
  that the selected bank will offer sufficient credit limits for the
  Group.
- New bank relations for subsidiaries
  When setting up an overlay or local bank concept, many subsidiaries can maintain their existing bank. This will make life
  a lot easier for them. Most subsidiaries will probably find it
  positive to work with a local bank with well known systems
  and local support. On the other hand, when a global cash
  pool is selected, a request for proposal ought to be sent to
  local banks in order to establish an efficient local cash pool.
  This implies that a change of local bank supplier could take
  place as well, even though the local or overlay concept is
  selected.
- Cost
  As mentioned earlier, large volumes enhance the negotiation power and influence the total cost for the cash pool set

up. However, it is possible to achieve very good costs for the local and overlay alternatives as well, but it will be time consuming to negotiate prices with a larger number of banks.

- Counter party exposure
  When selecting a single bank, the counter party exposure dramatically increases. During the entire day, the total liquidity risk is in one bank. The local and overlay concepts reduce this risk to only a limited part of the day, and if daily deposits are made from the global cash pool this risk is further reduced.

- Manual sweeps
  Depending on the banks to be included in the local and overlay set up, there will be more or less manual transfers to be executed on a daily basis. Manual sweeps can be totally avoided with a single bank set-up. Manual sweeps will cause additional work and reduce the efficiency of the cash pool.

- Number of accounts
  Bank accounts are expensive to keep and maintain. It is not only the cost per account to the bank but the internal costs for accounting and reconciliation that have to be considered. The number of accounts will increase with an overlay concept.

- Local banking capabilities
  Although the large international banks operate as local banks in many of the Euro countries, in many cases their provision of local services will not meet the standards of the strongest local banks. Services such as petty cash, cashing of cheques and execution of salary payments are often better managed by a local domestic bank.

Conclusion

As discussed earlier, the most likely solution will be a mixed concept including the single, overlay and local cash pool concepts. A mixed concept will meet the objective to pool the liquidity of the

Group since daily transfers will be executed. This solution is flexible and offers strategic alternatives for the subsidiaries to choose among. When requested by the subsidiaries, the local bank can be kept, and when this is not necessary, the global bank could be selected.

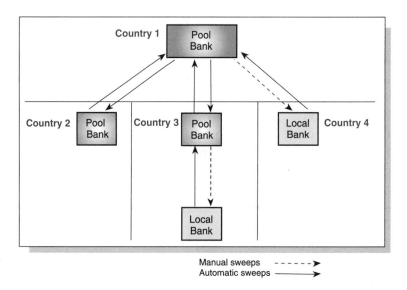

Mixed concept − single + overlay + local bank

In a perfect world, all balances are automatically transferred to the global pool. When this is not possible to achieve, aspects such as increased administration should be considered. Perhaps is it a better solution to leave target balances on the local accounts and only transfer to the global pool when the balance is above a local maximum balance. Another solution is to make regular transfers — for example once a week — from the local to the global pool.

This kind of mixed pool will technically be easy to implement, but in practice, when there are a number of different banks involved, it could be a challenge. Many agreements with different banks have to be negotiated, not only between the Group and the local banks but also between the Global and local banks. This solution will most likely take somewhat longer to implement, and the cost for the total pool will increase compared to the single bank concept.

An example of a real life solution: A combination of three banks, an overlay structure, zero balance and notional pooling

Toshiba International Finance have chosen to work with three banks to pool Toshiba's European cash. The two currencies which are pooled are Euro and Sterling.

Toshiba opened a Euro master account located in the UK. Overlay accounts were opened for branches in Paris, Düsseldorf, Amsterdam and London. These accounts are zero balanced through cross border sweeps to the master account.

As there are a number of different companies in Germany, the Euro balances in Germany are locally zero balanced before they are swept to the master account in the UK.

The intention is to create a separate international Euro cash pool with another bank for an international division with head office in the Netherlands. The balance from that pool will also be transferred to the overlay bank and swept to the UK master account.

Finally, a third bank is used to notionally pool all Toshiba's Sterling balances in the UK.

Once the total vision, including pooling technique as well as bank concept is set, this can be communicated both internally and externally. When the subsidiaries have been involved in creating the solution, the decision will most likely be well received in the organisation. There is now a mutual vision as to how the Group's cash management will be managed in the future. The next step is to explain the vision in detail and send out a request for proposal to the banks in question.

8

ACTIVE LIQUIDITY MANAGEMENT

INTRODUCTION

An important part of the day to day cash management effort will be to actively manage cash balances and foreign exchange cash flow. In this chapter we will discuss the basic reasons and methods for forecasting and managing liquidity. First, we will discuss liquidity forecasting and planning, on a short term and on a longer term. Thereafter, we will discuss the advantages of matching foreign currency cash flow. We will not, however, develop the closely related and important topics of foreign exchange and interest risk management. Those topics are vast and complex enough to merit a book of their own!

LIQUIDITY FORECASTING AND PLANNING

Short term liquidity forecasting is performed in order to manage short term liquidity fluctuations optimally and to be able to ensure that sufficient liquidity reserves are always available. Well functioning procedures for liquidity forecasting contribute to the company's ability to adapt to any situation which may arise in the day-to-day activities of the company.

Long term liquidity management is performed in order to enable decisions regarding longer term financing and investments.

Short term liquidity management

Short term liquidity management usually comprises a monthly forecast one year ahead and a daily rolling forecast for the next 2–4 weeks ahead. The monthly planning aims to capture the seasonal liquidity fluctuations, such as invoicing perhaps being lower the month following the holiday period in service companies, the reduction of sales in the winter for the ice-cream company, or the reduction of cash flow in the summer in skiing resorts. The more cyclical the cash flow of the company is, the more important it will be to carefully forecast and monitor the liquidity levels of the company.

Be appropriately ambitious

Which cash flow should be included in your forecast?

Does every company in a large Group have to be included in the cash flow forecast of a large corporation? Our answer is no. Particularly if you utilise a cash pooling structure with reasonable possibilities for subsidiaries to cover short term liquidity requirements with credits on their pool accounts. Efficient short term liquidity forecasting must concentrate on the large streams of cash flow. If certain companies in the Group are so small that their cash flow does not have any significant impact on the total liquidity position of the Group, there is no need to ask these entities to report.

Nor do you need to capture every detail of the cash flow of the larger entities. What is important is to capture their significant cash streams. Certain items in the cash flow forecast will almost always be very uncertain, particularly on the receipt side. Over time, the persons who perform the cash flow forecast will learn to interpret the information which is gathered, and form a relatively correct opinion on how much of the receipts due on a particular date are likely to arrive on that day. Therefore, there is no point wasting the organisation's resources on forecasting insignificant cash movements. If you spend a reasonable time to capture the most significant streams, you will have successfully completed your assignment.

Should the account balances always be managed to 0?

Theoretically, perfect liquidity management is to manage each bank account balance so that you have no interest bearing funds on account at the end of each day, but all surplus should be invested in higher yielding money market instruments or deficits covered by cheaper money market credits. Is that reasonable?

First of all, we recommend every corporation to keep negotiated credit lines against each cash account. This will enable you to *target* a zero balance, rather than the positive balance you will need to target if each negative balance is hit by expensive overdraft interest rates.

However, actually reaching a close to zero balance, if even that is possible, normally requires quite some effort. If the interest rate on the bank account/bank accounts is sufficiently close to the money market rate, it may not be justified to spend that effort to move the last balance out of the account. Indeed, several large corporations have managed to negotiate so beneficial interest rate conditions on the top accounts of their cash pools that they do not bother to invest or borrow on the money market at all!

> **Several large corporations have managed to negotiate so beneficial interest rate conditions on the top accounts of their cash pools that they do not bother to invest or borrow on the money market at all!**

A similar solution, equally attractive, is to arrange for an automatic transfer of the net balance on the account to or from a money market fund. This is a relatively new solution offered by a small number of banks. Most banks still have problems putting this solution in place in an automated fashion. We believe this is a very attractive product, however, and that it is likely to rapidly gain market share.

Certain corporations decide that it is simply too hard to manage each currency on a same day basis every morning, i.e. calculate the cash available for investment or required to borrow and execute the deals before cut-off time for a number of currencies. These corporations manage only their most important currencies on a same day basis and manage the remaining currencies on a "+1 basis", i.e. allow a balance equivalent to one day's transactions to remain on the bank account for one day and manage that balance the next day. If this is the chosen method, usually it will be combined with negotiating reasonable interest rates on the bank accounts and not be particularly costly, while allowing the treasury department to spread their work load over the entire day, instead of doing the majority of the work early in the morning.

Each company will need to perform their own calculation to establish which is the appropriate strategy for their situation. Many corporations will find that targeting a zero bank account balance is, indeed, feasible and profitable, whilst others will come to the conclusion that slightly lowering the ambition is more cost efficient.

Cut-off times

As mentioned above, the cut-off times for same day value clearing of transactions will determine the ability to actively manage liquidity balances on a same day basis. These are also highly important to study when setting up zero balance pooling solutions. In order to be able to manage bank accounts to a zero balance, all commercial and financial payments with value of the relevant day need to be reported on your account prior to making the payment related to the daily money market investment.

Cut-off times vary between countries and between banks. They are almost always negotiable between the bank and the customer. The reason for that is that whilst the clearing system will have a specific cut-off time after which the banks can no longer process transactions, the bank will always demand a margin for the time the bank needs to process payment instructions received from customers. The standard cut-off time offered by the bank will therefore be somewhat longer than that which the bank may accept from a preferred customer.

Clearing is an area which is currently rapidly developing and becoming increasingly competitive, as several clearing hubs for the Euro have developed. (Read more about clearing in chapter 5: *Clearing, payments and receipts*.) One important trend is that clearing times are extending to later and later in the day and that clearing is often performed at several different times within the day.

Procedures

In order to be able to perform the short term liquidity forecast, you need procedures for gathering the relevant information. Here is a suggestion of how you may want to structure procedures enabling the gathering of the necessary information for your liquidity forecast.

- Daily information on the opening liquidity position of each day should be easily obtained from your electronic banking terminal. Note, that you need *the net balance of available funds*, as opposed to the total of transactions booked on the account. This will be particularly important in those countries where drafts and other forward dated payment instruments are frequent. Something else which may make it difficult to optimise your balance utilisation is if your bank makes frequent corrections of value dates on your account. If this happens regularly, it will be difficult or impossible to keep optimised accounts.
- Expected monthly payments and receipts are gathered from each company or unit for one year ahead. Often, this information is gathered at the same time as the budget information. Note that the information should always be structured *per currency* to be paid or received. Thereby, you can utilise the same forecast for liquidity and foreign currency exposure management.

> **The information should always be structured *per currency* to be paid or received. Thereby, you can utilise the same forecast for liquidity and foreign currency exposure management.**

- Each forecast is updated regularly. This may be on a weekly or a monthly basis, depending on what suits your company and to what degree you are able to automate the forecast.
- Any significant deviations from the forecast should be immediately reported to the central treasury unit, if the amount is large enough to impact the total liquidity position of the Group.

Case: Real estate company within the Group

A mortgage bank we worked with owned a real estate company. The treasury department of the mortgage bank was always annoyed with the real estate company, which would regularly sell or buy commercial properties without giving prior notice to the treasury department. Whenever this happened, the liquidity forecast was way off and the treasury department was unable to optimise the Group liquidity position.

We helped the Group to put in place a simple cash pool, where the real estate company got access to a generous credit limit and financing directly over the bank account at favourable conditions, but only as long as they reported liquidity forecasts on a weekly basis and gave prompt updates as soon as a new real estate deal was coming up. The management of the real estate company was delighted with this simple arrangement and from day-to-day they would call the treasury department of the mortgage bank and provide updates on the probability of each deal coming through and on what day the settlement was likely to take place.

Sources of cash flow

The main sources of cash flow to be captured in the short term liquidity forecast are the following:

Operative cash flow		Possible to forecast
Receipts	Customer receipts	Partly
Payments	Salaries	Yes
	Payment of goods and services	Yes
	Tax	Yes
	Interest	Yes
	Amortisation	Yes
	Dividends	Yes
	Other	Partly

Operative cash flow		
Financial cash flow	+ expiring investments	Yes
	− expiring loans	Yes
	+ existing loans	Yes
	− existing investments	Yes

Today's surplus or deficit		

This table shows that, in fact, most payments are possible to forecast, but that it is more difficult to forecast the receipts. How well you manage to forecast your receipts will largely depend on the following parameters:

- What type of business are you in? Do you sell large projects with a few large invoices, or do you regularly send many small invoices?
- Do you deliver goods regularly or periodically?
- Which are your payment terms? If, for example, your payment conditions state free delivery month plus 30 days credit, you can easily forecast that the majority of your payments will arrive concentrated to a few days at the end of the month and the first few days of the next month. If you have a payment condition like 10 days net invoice, your cash flow will depend

on how frequently you ship goods and, of course, of the payment moral of your customers.

The benefits of active liquidity planning

The results of active liquidity planning are:

- Efficient bank balance management
  — By actively managing the balances you keep on account, a comparison of the conditions on different bank accounts can lead to savings.
- Investment of temporary cash surplus or loans to cover temporary deficits at better interest rate
  — By being aware of which amounts and during which periods you will need to make investments or loans, you can obtain better conditions. The company can then turn to the money market or invest/borrow from the bank at better conditions than if utilising the normal bank account.
  — The interest differential between a normal corporate bank account and the money market is usually approximately 0.5%. Furthermore, overnight (O/N) investments are capitalised every day. This is particularly interesting in times or markets of high interest rates. At an interest level of 10%, this gives a further return of approximately 0.5% per year. If, however, the interest rate level is lower, say 3%, this effect is significantly lower and equal to 0.05%.
  — The total difference between an overnight investment and a passive investment on a regular bank account is approximately 0.5–1% per year. When financing a deficit, the difference is smaller, as the bank will usually capitalise the interest on a loan more frequently than on an investment. Therefore, it may be interesting to borrow on your bank account at the start of an interest period, as the interest will not be capitalised until the end of the period.

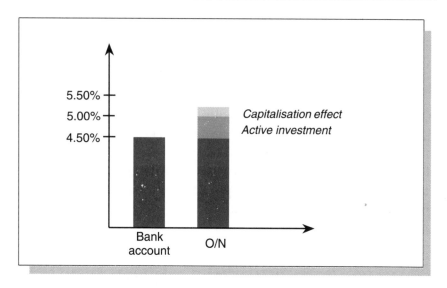

Interest differential, investment O/N or on bank account

Automation

Most modern treasury workstations provide the capability for monitoring daily liquidity position and simulating the effects of planned financing or investment alternatives. If your treasury workstation does not have a good functionality for this, or indeed, you operate without such a tool, it is also relatively easy to build a model for this on your PC.

It is standard practise to keep an automated link between the ledgers of financial assets and debts into the liquidity forecasting tool, to manage and forecast which financial assets and debts mature on each day.

If you desire a highly integrated systems environment, you can also build interfaces from your accounts payable and accounts receivable ledgers into your liquidity forecasting tool. This will, of course, be easier to do if you have a uniform systems environment throughout the Group, so that the same interface can be utilised for each company which is connected to the forecasting tool. Some of the modern ERP systems offer cash management modules which perform this as standard functionality.

Long term liquidity forecasting

The purpose of the long term liquidity forecast is to provide management with information for long term decisions, such as determining the required level of liquidity reserves, optimising the capital structure of the balance sheet, as regards leverage and structure of financing as well as providing information regarding investment and acquisition decisions.

Liquidity reserves

The required level of liquidity reserves should be stated in the treasury policy of each company. This can be stated as a nominal figure or as a percentage of a particular parameter which is relevant to the specific company. One examples is: "Liquidity reserves should cover all payments in the next three months." Certain companies prefer to keep liquidity reserves proportionate to a certain percentage of the loans due to expire over the next 6 months. Another example is to maintain liquidity reserves equal to a certain percentage of the turnover.

Again, each company will need to make their own definition of what they consider to be liquid assets. Most consider cash on account and committed credit lines as assets which are definitely liquid. They then come into the more arbitrary formulation: "Assets which can be sold in a liquid market." This is where you will need to make a judgement. Most money market instruments which are traded in a market with small spreads between buy and sell prices can be considered to be liquid. These are usually government issued securities, but sometimes also corporate debt issues.

Some companies will consider uncommitted credit lines as part of their liquidity. We generally would not recommend that. If your bank relationships are currently such that an uncommitted credit line is considered as safe as a committed line, this may completely change the moment you really need your liquidity reserves.

> **If your bank relationships are currently such that an uncommitted credit line is considered as safe as a committed line, this may completely change the moment you really need your liquidity reserves**

Performing your long term liquidity forecast

Long term liquidity planning is normally performed 3 to 5 years forward. The main difference between short term and long term liquidity planning is that when planning with a longer horizon, you need to consider more uncertain parameters, such as price changes to customers and from suppliers, demand fluctuations for your products or services, salary increases as well as macro economic parameters such as interest rates and inflation.

Performing long term liquidity planning makes it necessary to make assumptions about the future. Therefore, this activity is best performed using a simulation model where it is easy to make changes to the assumptions and simulate different scenarios.

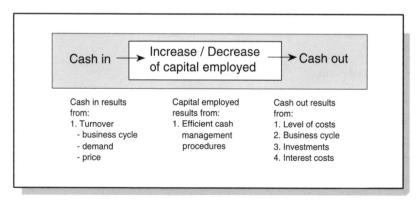

Long term liquidity forecasting

Sources of cash flow

The long term liquidity forecast contains the same elements as the short term liquidity forecast, but when simulating the long term liquidity it is usually easier to utilise traditional cash flow analysis, starting with the balance sheet and the profit and loss statement, see an example below.

Cash flow analysis		% of revenue
Sales	1 000	100
Cost of goods sold	600	60
Gross profit	**400**	**40**
Salaries	−100	10
Operational costs	−75	7.5
Other costs	−25	2.5
Profit before depreciation	**200**	**20**
− Tax	−54	
+/− accounts receivable	50	
+/− accounts payable	25	
+/− stock	−20	
Operative cash flow	**201**	
+/− debts	50	
+/− financial profit	−5	
+/− dividends	−10	
− investments	−400	
Funding requirement	**−164**	

The analysis usually starts with the sales projections. Thereafter, the costs are calculated based on last year's cost level, with an assumption about price development and the projected production volume.

You then deduct salaries, operational costs, such as electricity, rent and marketing, and other costs. The result is a forecast of the profit before depreciation. After adjusting for tax payments and changes to the accounts receivable and payable and stock you obtain the operative cash flow. If you then adjust for the increase or decrease in debts, the financial result, dividends and planned investments, the funding requirement of the company is projected.

MATCHING OF CASH FLOW IN FOREIGN CURRENCY

For companies with frequent receipts and payments of a certain foreign currency, it may be advantageous to open a bank account in that currency, instead of converting the currency at each transaction. You can then utilise your receipts to make payments in the same currency.

The advantages of matching currency flows are:

- The company avoids converting foreign currency against its base currency. The banks will charge a margin for each conversion, which over time makes this expensive.
- There is no currency risk for that part of the cash flow which is perfectly matched, i.e. the volume of receipts which is immediately used for payments.

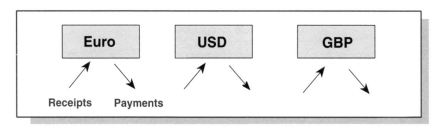

Currency accounts

The more you have centralised your account structure, the higher your matching opportunity will be. Thus, pooling your accounts will also give you this additional benefit!

Timing differences managed with swaps

If there are timing differences between receipts and payments, these can be resolved in the following manner, for example. Assume the company receives a payment in USD and that an equivalent amount is to be paid out one month later.

The received USD payment is converted at spot rate to your local currency, assume this is GBP. At the same time, a forward transaction is performed, i.e. you repurchase the USD with a forward value at fixed price for the day in which the currency will be required for your payment. This is called making a swap. Your GBP are available to your British operations during a month and can then be used again for the USD payment. Note: When you purchase this transaction from the bank, make sure to ask for a swap, not for a spot and a forward deal, otherwise you will lose out on the spreads!

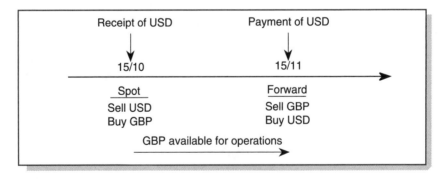

Currency swap

SUMMARY

Key points to remember about active liquidity management

1. Concentrate the cash flow forecast on the significant cash movements of the Group.
2. Evaluate whether it will be more beneficial for you to manage each bank account to a close to zero balance each day or if it is more cost effective to leave some balances on bank accounts.
3. Negotiate credit lines on every important bank account.
4. Try to negotiate a close to money market interest rate on the top account of your cash pool/s.
5. Efficient short term liquidity forecasting requires fixed procedures and regular reporting.
6. Structure your short term liquidity forecast per currency. Thereby you can utilise the same forecast for liquidity and FX exposure management.
7. Active liquidity management controls your liquidity risk and improves your net interest profit/loss.
8. The liquidity forecast can be highly automated.
9. Long term liquidity forecasting enables optimisation of your balance sheet and planning for investments and acquisitions.
10. Matching of payments and receipts in foreign currencies avoids conversion cost and FX risk.
11. The more centralised your account structure is, the higher your matching opportunity will be.

9

FROM VISION TO CONTRACT

INTRODUCTION

This chapter will discuss two phases; creating the vision and selection of bank. The steps in these phases will be analysed and methods on how to come up with a vision and to select a future baking partner will be presented.

CREATING THE VISION

A vision should guide every major project. A vision is a strategic high level decision of the final result of the project. This strategic vision must be sponsored by top management and have the support of the entire organisation. Without a clear vision, there is a risk of delayed projects, project members striving towards different solutions and misunderstandings, all together ending up in something not in line with the top management strategy.

It is well worth spending time during this first phase of the project, since with a well founded and accepted vision, substantial time savings will be gained later during the procurement and implementation phases.

In this section, the following different steps in the process of creating a Euro cash pool vision for an international Group will be discussed:

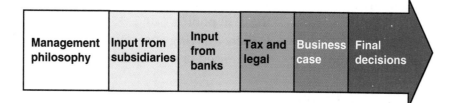

Phase 1–Creating the vision

Management philosophy

To start with, the general strategic philosophy of the company should be outlined. A vision not in line with the management philosophy is not worth working with.

An example of a strategic decision is whether Treasury within the Group should be a centralised or decentralised function. With a centralised strategy, decisions about, for example, foreign exchange, short term funding/investment and cash management will most likely be made by Group Treasury. With a decentralised strategy, these decisions are all made locally. When selecting between a single, overlay or local bank strategy, information about management philosophy is vital.

With the introduction of the Euro, there are also other important aspects to consider which previously were not there. Now, it is possible to co-ordinate the flows for a number of countries and take advantage of the economies of scale from the pooling effects and increased negotiation power.

The following aspects, described more thoroughly in chapter 6: *Introduction to cash pooling*, have to be considered when creating the vision for an international cash pool:

- Organisation   Manufacturing or sales company?
- Banks   Keep the existing or select a new bank?
                    One or several banks?
- IT-structure   Complexity of IT within the company?

- Countries   Which countries should participate in
                           the cash pool?
- Cash flow structure   Is there a savings potential?
- Type of company   Centralised or decentralised company?

Input from subsidiaries

Even with a centralised treasury strategy, it is important to involve the subsidiaries in the vision phase. The subsidiaries will later be the final users and would therefore have to add their views and raise demands on the vision. Without a general commitment and consensus from the subsidiaries, it will be difficult, later on during the project, to implement the selected vision.

The major subsidiaries should be visited by the project group. During these meetings, the objective of the project can be explained and the specific individual requirements by the subsidiary obtained. Moreover, information about the current banks and bank accounts and copies of the existing bank agreements can be collected. Many subsidiaries will not have any detailed agreements in place but are working on the basis of the general conditions. In these general conditions, the float is hardly ever obvious to the reader but needs to be examined in further detail. Direct contact with the bank is the only way to receive this information.

The result of the visits to subsidiaries can be summarised as follows:

- The objective of the project is explained
- Requirements from the subsidiaries are collected
- Information about current banks is gained
- Existing bank agreements are collected
- Cash flow information is received

This is the part of the project which most companies underestimate. Involvement takes time and is costly, but it is an investment for future savings.

Tax and legal

No cash pool structure can be implemented before tax and legal considerations are thoroughly penetrated. During the vision phase, this can only be done on a comprehensive level. A more thorough investigation must be made when procurement and implementation starts. Even though the bank is not responsible for these evaluations, the companies expect to receive basic information about tax and legal restrictions for each country concerned from the bank. The companies have to use local and international experts on tax and legal questions in order to make sure that they will comply to the rules in the different countries.

The tax and legal area is complicated, but not impossible. A structured approach simplifies this process. Examples of different tax and legal issues that need to be penetrated are discussed in chapter 6: *Introduction to cash pooling*.

Input from banks

When creating a vision, it is important to be updated on new bank products, systems currently in place and solutions planned to be developed by the banks. One way to get this input is to invite some of the relevant banks for a presentation of their products and what is in the pipeline within the near future. This is also an opportunity to evaluate which banks will receive a Request for Proposal (RFP) during the final procurement phase.

Another way of gaining this information is to visit seminars frequently arranged on this topic or to visit other companies and discuss it with them.

Creating a business case

One of the first questions always asked when discussing changes is "how much will we save on this"? In most companies several projects are in the pipeline to start somewhere within the near future. The better a well defined savings potential can be explained to top management, the higher attention the project will get. Without a clear answer on the savings potential, it is not very likely that there will be any changes at all.

The savings potential can be estimated in a business case. A business case will compare current costs and fees for payment and cash management services with the expected costs for the planned future vision. The total yearly savings potential in a business case can be divided into four main areas:

- Payments; incoming and outgoing, international and domestic
- Pooling effects
- Other bank fees
- Foreign exchange (FX) transactions

Payments

From the subsidiaries which are to be included in a future Euro cash pool, the number of domestic and international payments, the costs for making the transactions and the float should be collected. This information is put in a spread sheet where the total actual cost for the payments in all countries is calculated. In order to calculate an estimated savings potential, reference conditions for future float and costs are used. The reference conditions will reflect the negotiation power and the possible changed payment methods and techniques to be used in the new set up.

Pooling effects

When calculating the pooling effect, the daily cash balance statements from the subsidiaries to be included in the cash pool are analysed. The value date balances should be used since they are the actual interest bearing balances on the accounts. This information can sometimes be difficult to receive from the banks. For certain banks there might be a need to approximate this information.

To start with, the average daily positive or negative balances are calculated per account and subsidiary. When pooling per country takes place, a savings potential per country is calculated. Thereafter, all local balances are added and netted in order to calculate the total pooling effect.

In addition to the pooling effect, the savings calculation will reflect assumptions of improved interest rate conditions for both positive and negative balances.

Other bank fees

Other bank fees — such as fees for electronic banking, bank account statements and maintenance — are also analysed. When settling a Euro cash pool concept, these costs are likely to be reduced. How much will depend on the final bank concept selected. When selecting a single bank concept, other bank fees will probably be less expensive than when selecting a local bank concept. However, by sending out a well structured Request For Proposal (RFP) both concepts will probably add on to the total savings potential.

FX transactions

Savings potential occurs when most FX transactions are made with one single bank or through Group Treasury. Substantial savings can be achieved by negotiating favourable standard margins for international payments. The savings potential for FX transactions includes the FX transactions between Euro and other non-Euro currencies such as for example British pounds,

Japanese yen, US dollars and Swedish, Danish and Norwegian Krona.

This savings potential is not dependent on a Euro cash pool but can be achieved as a single project. However, it is natural to discuss this potential in this context since the change of FX routines is closely related to the account and payment structure and selection of bank.

A model for presentation

Below, an example of the final table for presentation is outlined. Since the FX transaction related savings are not really dependent on a Euro cash pool solution, but can be realised independantly, there are two levels of savings in the table.

Potential savings

Euro currencies	Fee	Float	Total
Incoming payments			
Outgoing payments			
Pooling effects			
Other bank fees			
Subtotal			
FX-transactions			
Total			

In addition to these savings, there will most likely be rationalisation potentials in the subsidiaries. When introducing new ways of working and new procedures, the different processes for payments and cash management in the individual subsidiaries can most likely be improved. However, this saving is often difficult to estimate at this stage.

There is also a cost for the implementation that has to be considered and estimated. The pay off for the project (savings divided by implementation costs) should be calculated and presented to the top management.

The final decision

Based on the information collected during the project, i.e. management philosophy, meetings with banks and subsidiaries, tax and legal as well as the analysis of payments, pooling effect, other bank fees and FX-transactions, the final vision can be decided.

It is advisable that the top management of the Group is involved in the final decision making workshop. Top management commitment for the project will be needed during the procurement and implementation phase.

Most companies are looking for a simple and realistic vision which is easy to implement. Time is money and cash management savings are annual repetitive savings. A delay of a couple of months during the implementation phase is a lost savings potential.

> **Time is money; a delayed implementation is a lost savings potential**

During the visioning workshop, a vision of how the Group should work with payments and cash management in the near future is created. The functionality of the solution is closely scrutinised. It is important that the vision will work in an efficient way for the subsidiaries and be looked upon as an improvement compared to the actual solutions.

When creating a vision, decisions about the following areas should be taken

- The role of subsidiaries/ Group Treasury

  Evaluation of subsidiaries before or after financial net?

- FX management

  Centralised or decentralised FX management?

- Cash pooling technique

  Zero balance, notional pooling or single legal account pooling techniques?

- Cross border pooling technique

  The combination of pooling techniques cross border and pooling per entity or per country?

- Payment structure

  How are internal and external payments to be settled by the subsidiaries?

- Bank concept

  Single, overlay or local bank concept?

- Countries to be included

  Which countries are to be included in the Euro cash pool.

In order for top management and the Treasury department to communicate the vision to banks and internally within the Group, it is advisable to present a schematic picture of the vision as well as bullet points of the future main functionality of the pool.

Once the vision is agreed upon, the second phase can start, i.e. the procurement of supplier for the service.

Case: Large European company with a turnover of 10 000 M EUR

The company started its Euro cash pool project by having initial meetings with several international and local banks. The banks briefly presented their abilities regarding Euro cash pooling. The company estimated it would take a few months to select a bank.

When receiving the proposals from the banks it became apparent that the offers from the banks differed in scope and detail, and it was impossible for the company to select a Euro cash pool bank based on the answers. At this stage, consultants were asked to help evaluate the bank offers.

When analysing the RFP, it showed that it did not clearly specify the company's vision for its Euro cash pool or inform about the legal structure and current cash flows. It was also very weak in discussing pooling techniques, bank solutions (single bank, overlay, or local bank), tax and legal issues etc. Furthermore, it lacked detailed questions regarding prices, other charges, interest calculation and allocation, payments/receipts, sweeps, training and implementation etc.

The vision was clarified, additional information requested from the banks, and the bank offers evaluated from both a qualitative and quantitative perspective. The Euro cash pool bank was selected more than one year after the initial meetings were held with the banks.

THE REQUEST FOR PROPOSAL AND SELECTION OF BANK

Once the vision is set, the work with a Request For Proposal (RFP) to the banks can start. In this second phase, the following steps can be identified:

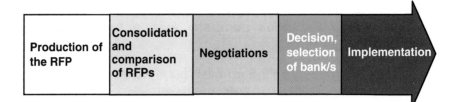

| Production of the RFP | Consolidation and comparison of RFPs | Negotiations | Decision, selection of bank/s | Implementation |

Phase 2–Selection of bank/s

How many banks and which banks should receive an RFP? The answer to this question is not always that easy. It is important to bear in mind that it takes considerable time for the banks to write the proposals and for the project team to evaluate them.

Between 3–5 banks must be considered a reasonable amount. If it is a simple, straight forward standard solution for a Group not too large, it is probably enough with three banks. For a somewhat more complicated solution for a large Group, maybe as many as five banks could be considered.

> **It takes considerable time for the banks to write the proposals and for the project team to evaluate them**

One way of reducing the number of banks to receive an RFP is to first send out a Request For Information (RFI) to a larger number of banks. An RFI will ask for information about the banks ability to deliver certain basic solutions needed by the Group. After the evaluation of the RFI, the number of banks to receive the RFP can be reduced.

When selecting the banks to receive an RFP, there are many different aspects which need to be considered. Should the current cash management banks be included? Should it be a new bank for the Group offering advanced payment and cash pool solutions? Historic relationship as well as functionality are also important aspects. The bank must be prepared to respond and act quickly and take risks on the Group when needed. In order for a large Group to select a new banking partner there has to be a very strong commitment displayed from top management within the bank.

When making the final selection of cash management bank, both quantitative as well as qualitative aspects must be considered. These will be discussed further on page 175: *Evaluation, consolidation and comparison of RFPs.*

Contents of an RFP

When writing an RFP, it is of utmost importance to be clear, precise and to present the necessary information needed by the bank. The better the RFP is, the easier it will be for the bank to write an offer, and fewer questions will have to be asked.

To start with, an RFP should contain a very short and executive introduction including the following information:

Background of the project

The executive introduction will most likely be read by many bankers not previously involved with the Group. A short background of why the project has started and some information about the Group is therefore necessary.

Cash management vision set by the Group

An overview of the vision set by the Group should be given. The objective is to briefly inform the reader of the final cash management vision.

The content of the RFP

In order for the reader to know what is to come in the RFP, a short and informative description is always helpful. The expected content of the received proposal from the bank can be listed. By listing this information early on in the RFP, the bank can allocate the correct resources when writing the proposal.

Reference persons within the company for further questions

Even though there have been meetings between the Group and the bank, and the RFP has been written with great care, there are always further questions which the bank would like to ask. In order to simplify, for both the bank and the project team, the correct names, telephone and fax numbers as well as e-mail addresses should be given to the people to whom the questions should be addressed. By giving this information, the questions will be addressed to the correct individuals and the response will be fast and accurate. In this way, the overview and control of the project is also maintained by the project team.

When a lot of subsidiaries are included in an RFP for a Group, local personnel are not always aware of the details in the vision and should therefore not be addressed by the bank. This could also cause confusion within the Group, create unnecessary misunderstandings and delay the project.

Response format

In order for the project team to accurately and efficiently evaluate proposals from different banks, it is of utmost importance that the banks follow a structured response format. This format should be briefly explained in the introduction.

Time table for the RFP and the implementation

In order for the bank to give the correct priority and to allocate the correct number of resources for the proposal, the timetable for the RFP and the implementation should be given. This is vital information for the bank. If the bank is prepared to respond to the RFP, it must also be prepared to deliver on time.

All these elements taken together, will give the readers a better understanding of the RFP and what the Group is expecting to receive from the bank. After this short and executive introduction the detailed RFP can be introduced.

The detailed RFP

The objective of the detailed RFP is to provide the bank with all necessary information needed to be able to write a proposal to the Group and to ask all relevant questions necessary for the evaluation. Once again, the vision will be explained but this time in further detail. This section will briefly explain the information needed in the detailed RFP.

Global pooling method

The pooling techniques to be used per country and on a global level are explained as well as the frequency and level of automisation of the funding/withdrawal to/from the sub accounts. To avoid misunderstandings, it is always helpful to communicate with a picture of the final set-up. Below, an example of an overlay set-up with local banks and weekly manual sweeps is described.

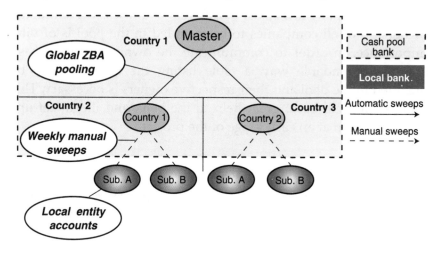

Example of a global cash pool set-up

Number of accounts

The RFP should include a list of future accounts per entity, specifying in which countries the accounts should be located. An easy way of communicating this is to set up a matrix with all entities to be included in the pool and the countries where the account is to be opened.

Interest calculation and inter company loans

Interest will always be calculated and allocated to the Group on the pooled balance. However, this is not enough for Groups using the zero balance pooling technique. With this technique a number of daily inter company loans will occur. In order for the Group to reconcile the loans, the banks will have to offer a shadow administration where the Group can follow the individual internal balances and set internal interest rates. This has to be explained and later on evaluated in detail since all banks cannot provide this kind of service. If this cannot be offered by the bank, it has to be managed internally by the Group.

Legal structure

Different company laws exist in different countries. Therefore, the ownership of all companies to be included in the pool is of vital importance. In order to communicate the ownership in an easy and understandable way, a table listing the companies to be included in the pool and their respective owners is necessary. This information will be of great help to the bank and illegal set-ups can be avoided at an early stage of the project.

Legal structure

Country	Company	Owner	Ownership	Nationality of owner
France	XYZ S.A.	ABC, GmbH	100 %	German

Electronic banking system

One important criteria when selecting a bank, is the quality and efficiency of the Electronic Banking (EB) system. In order to evaluate the offers, the technical as well as functional requirements on the EB-systems should be listed in the RFP. Below, some general requirements are listed;

- Payments can be initiated from an accounts payable or a treasury system and imported into the application.
- The system can handle local standard payments.
- Repetitive payments can be pre-defined in templates for easier initiation.
- The system can provide book balances and value date balances.
- Choice of language in the system.
- Easy to define new reports without need for additional programming.

It is not always necessary for a Group to have the latest EB-system developed on the market. Many of the recently developed functions might not be necessary for all Groups. But even if all EB functions are not needed today, it should be an active decision by the Group not to use the function and not simply because the bank cannot provide it. Even if a function is not needed today it might be needed in the near future.

Number of transactions and volumes

In order for the bank to present a price for payments, information about the expected number of transactions and volumes split per currency and country and per financial and commercial flows is vital. Without this information, the bank will not be able to make a business case on the Group. It makes a substantial difference for the bank if there will be many small payments or a few large ones. If this information is not provided, most likely, the pricing will be higher since the bank will have to estimate the numbers on their own and need to add a margin to cover that risk. A table with a useful layout for the expected number of transactions and flows is presented below.

FLOWS	Number of transactions	M Euro
Cross border payments / incoming		
Financial payments	300	40
Commercial payments	500	5
Cheques	200	2
Domestic payments / incoming		
Financial payments	50	10
Commercial payments	5 000	50
Cheques	500	1
TOTAL	**6 550**	**108**
Cross border payments / outgoing		
Financial payments	300	40
Commercial payments	400	4
Domestic payments / outgoing		
Financial payments	50	10
Commercial payments	4 000	40
TOTAL	**4 750**	**94**

Expected number of transactions and flows

Payment processing

In the next section, a detailed description of how the Group will receive and execute payments is presented. The set-up of both domestic and international payments should be described, as well as how the information to and from the bank should be transmitted. Various payment alternatives are described in further detail in chapter 6: *Clearing, payments and receipts.*

Security

The handling of electronic information and payment processing will need well developed security features within the bank. Therefore, security related questions must be included in the detailed questionnaire.

Regulatory reporting

How the banks provide service for automated regulatory reporting should also be raised. Automated reporting will be appreciated by the subsidiaries and save the Group a lot of valuable time. In most cases, the required information already exists in the systems of the bank and can be provided electronically to the Group or to the final receiver of the report.

Training

When setting up a new cash pool and cash management structure, the subsidiaries will need a lot of assistance and training from the bank. A description of how this will be made and the resources available at the bank is well worth asking for at this stage.

Day-to-day operations and back-up

All participating subsidiaries will need information on accurate balances and payments in progress. How this will be communicated and how errors will be corrected is vital information to receive in the proposal.

In the event of systems failure, the bank must have a back-up system in place. A description of the procedures in case of a breakdown of the banks mainframe or electronic banking tool is needed.

Branch network and partner banks

A relevant question from the Group and its subsidiaries is where the bank is represented through branches and partner banks. The language question within the branches should also be discussed as well as the level of support.

Support and availability are amongst the most important questions for the subsidiaries in the Group. If this is not satisfactory, the cash pool and cash management set-up will most likely fail.

General information

General information can be asked for. Examples of other areas which are included in the RFP are listed below.

- Credit risk rating of bank

    Moody's and/or Standard and Poor are the most common rating institutes to refer to.

- Implementation plan

    To ask the bank how the implementation will be made is valid information already at this point.

- References

    It is advisable to ask the bank for reference companies already using the bank's cash management services.

- Documentation

    Examples of documentation to be completed by the Group for account opening.

- Invoicing

    If the Group has any specific preferences regarding the invoicing from the bank, this can be mentioned in this section.

Detailed questionnaire

The detailed questionnaire will ask all relevant questions for the future cash pool and cash management set-up, including the areas listed above. All solutions, charges and conditions associated with different types of transactions, accounts or other services should be covered.

The banks should be asked to strictly follow the layout in the RFP when writing the offer. If this is not made, it is almost impossible to evaluate the offers from the different banks in a professional way. This should be pointed out when handing over the RFP to the banks. Many banks think it is time-consuming to answer the detailed questions but it is striking how often the banks have a hard time to come up with correct answers on simple and straight forward questions.

This is also the part of the RFP where detailed value dating conditions for different payments and receipts can be asked for. References to general terms and conditions in the standard contracts are unacceptable. The value dating rules should be explained in detail. One way of doing this is to use a table where the bank, for different payment types, will have to mark the booking dates, clearing date and value date. By doing this, the float will be obvious for the different payment types and will in the final evaluation be added as a cost.

In the example below there is a two day float for a S.W.I.F.T. standard payment. The bank withdraws the payment from the account of the paying company on the Tuesday, i.e. two days before it is actually sent to the clearing (Thursday).

For a 1 M Euro payment at an interest rate of 5%, a two day float of the payment is a cost for the Group and an earning for the bank of 278 Euro.

$$1\,000\,000 \text{ Euro} \times 2 \text{ days} / 360 \text{ days} \times 5\% = 278 \text{ Euro}$$

Example of a S.W.I.F.T. standard payment

Event/day	Monday	Tuesday	Wednesday	Thursday
Book keeping date	X			
Group value date		X		
Clearing date (the payment is executed by the bank)				X
Bank float		X	X	

In this section, all fees and charges for the cash pool and cash management set-up should appear and be explained by the bank in detail. Below, an exhibit from the detailed questionnaire regarding interest calculation is given.

Please state the offered interest rate on the global master account

_____

_____

_____

Please specify the number of interest bearing days per year

_____

_____

_____

Please specify the frequency of interest rate capitalisation

_____

Extract from a detailed questionnaire — interest calculation

The detailed questionnaire will take a lot of effort from the bank to fill in. Therefore, it is recommended to enclose the questionnaire on a floppy disk. The banks will then be able to fill in the questionnaire electronically and send it back in the original layout.

Presentation of the RFP

When the RFP is ready, it should be handed over to the banks. In order for the Group to describe the vision for the bank, avoid misunderstandings and to get a commitment from the start, a meeting where the RFP is handed over to the bank is recommended. The RFP could, of course, also be mailed to the bank.

In addition to this meeting, a second meeting can be set up during which the bank can ask additional questions. This meeting will assure the Group that the bank has understood the vision and will present a proposal to the Group.

Evaluation, consolidation and comparison of RFPs

When the proposals arrive, it is time to evaluate, consolidate and compare the bank proposals. One method to use when comparing the answers is to place all the questions in a table and fill in the answers from the respective banks. This can be done for both verbal and numeric answers. An example, the comparison of different interest rate conditions, is given below. The table shows a comparison of the offered interest rate conditions and frequency of capitalisation for three banks.

	A Bank	B Bank	C Bank
Interest conditions			
Interest base	Credit interest 365/365 Debet interest 360/365	365/360	360/360
Interest rate Credit balance	0-15 M EURO; EONIA - 30 BP	EONIA - 50 BP	EONIA - 10 BP
	>15 M EURO ; EONIA - 100 BP		
Debit balance	Euribor + 100 BP	EONIA + 50 BP	EONIA + 10 BP
Actual interest rate for amounts > 15 M EURO (EONIA = 3.05%)	2.05%	2.55%	2.95%
Frequency of interest capitalisation	Quarterly	Monthly	positive interest - yearly negative interest - monthly

Comparison of interest rate conditions

The calculation of interest of the total balance in the pool is normally related to a base rate. For the Euro, the banks normally refer to either EUONIA (Euro-zone Overnight Index Average Quote) or Euribor (Euro interbank offered rate). Those rates are calculated daily by the European Central Bank (ECB).

EUONIA is a weighted average of all overnight unsecured lending transactions in the inter bank market in the Euro area calculated on actual number of days over 360.

Euribor is calculated as EUONIA but using tomnext (tomorrow next), i.e. transactions 2 days ahead, for periods from 1 week to 12 months.

The interest can be expressed as for example EUONIA ± 50 BP (basis points). If EUONIA is 3%, this means that the interest on positive balances will be 2.5% and the interest on negative balances will be 3.5%. When different base rates are referred to, it means that the actual interest offered can vary between banks even though the margins are the same (i.e. ± 50 BP). When selecting a bank, it can be helpful to compare the base rates and evaluate the conditions based on the actual balance of the Group.

Most banks capitalise the interest once a year for positive balances, i.e. the interest is paid to the Group by the end of the year in December. However, for negative balances interest is capitalised somewhere between once a month to once a year. When comparing the conditions between different banks, the effective interest rate for the Group will have to be calculated also taking the capitalisation effect into account. The effective interest rate can be calculated with the following formula:

$$i = (1+R/m)^{(m \times n)}$$

i = Effective interest
R = Interest rate
m = Number of times the interest is capitalised
n = The number of years to be calculated for

Suppose that a 3% interest will be paid for 100 000 Euro during one year. Interest is capitalised four times per year. By using the above mentioned formula, the calculation will show that the 100 000 Euro will grow to $100\ 000 \times 1{,}0075^4 = 103\ 034$ Euro.

In the table below, the final total nominal amount plus interest at different capitalisation frequencies are given for the nominal amount of 100 000 Euro at an interest of 3%.

Capitalisation frequency 3% interest	100 000 EURO after 1 year
Yearly (m=1)	103 000
Half-yearly (m=2)	103 022
Quarterly (m=4)	103 034
Monthly (m=12)	103 042
Weekly (m=52)	103 045

Effect of the capitalisation frequency

The interest base used by the bank should also be looked into in further detail when evaluating a proposal. Is the interest calculated on the actual number of days 365/360, or 365/365 or as 30 days per month according to the formula 360/360? The difference between the interest rate basis is illustrated in the table below, still assuming a 3% interest.

Interest base	Investment amount	Interest
365/360	100 000 EURO	3 042 EURO
360/360	100 000 EURO	3 000 EURO
365/365	100 000 EURO	3 000 EURO

Yearly interest at different interest rate basis

A quantitative analysis of the prices for the offered cash pool and cash management services has to be made for each bank. If there are many different countries included in the cash pool, the cost analysis might have to be made per country and bank and then added together. The reason for this is that most banks do not have internal uniform pricing of the offered services across countries.

Different banks offer different ways of charging for their services. The most frequent areas to be included in the cost analysis are listed in the table below. The costs can be split into different cash pool costs, i.e. costs for setting up and using the cash pool, and in cost for flows.

Cash pool costs	Cost for flows
● Cash pool sweeps	● Local domestic payments
● Cash pool structure	
● Credit limits	● Cheque payments
● Interest rates	● Foreign payments financial commercial
● Number of terminals	
● Terminal information	● Guarantees
● Account information on file	● Salaries
● Other	

Example of costs to be included in the quantitative evaluation of proposals

Cash pool costs

In the cash pool costs, all cash pool related costs are listed, i.e., the cost for setting up the pool, the sweeps to and from the master account, the credit limit needed on the master account etc. The number of terminals and the information to be received on the terminal will also most likely be charged for.

Cost for flows

In this section, all payment related costs such as fees and float are calculated. Costs for guarantees and other types of special services, such as letters of credit, can be added in this section as well.

In order to get an overview of the proposals, a table including cash pool costs and cost for flows is made per bank. The table below shows an example of international payments and receipts. The information in the RFP regarding number of transfers and volumes will be used when calculating the total costs. Also included is the cost for float.

Payments	No. of transfers	MEURO	Fee /trans EURO	Total fee EURO	Float Days	Tot.cost of float EURO	Total Bank costs EURO
Cross border pmts. outgoing							
Financial pmts	300	40	10	3 000	0	0	3 000
Commercial pmts	400	4	10	4 000	1	467	4 467
Total	700	44		7 000		467	7 467
Cross border pmts. incoming							
Financial pmts	300	40	10	3 000	0	0	3 000
Commercial pmts	500	5	5	2 500	1	583	3 083
Cheques	200	2	10	2 000	5	833	2 833
Total	1 000	47		7 500		1 416	8 916
TOTAL				**14 500**		**1 833**	**16 383**

Analysis of fees and costs for cross border payments and receipts

When all the costs have been calculated and verified, the cost for the different banks can be summarised. In the table below, three banks are evaluated and the total bank cost split in fees and float can be seen. This table will serve as a first guide to the Group on how much the cash pool will cost and what the proposals from the different banks are worth. It will also answer whether the calculated savings in the previously made business case were correct.

Total bank costs	Bank A			Bank B			Bank C		
000 EURO	Fee	Float	Total	Fee	Float	Total	Fee	Float	Total
Total cost for flows	65	15	80	76	35	111	80	45	125
Total cash pool costs	60		60	36		36	36		36
Total bank costs	**125**	**15**	**140**	**112**	**35**	**147**	**116**	**45**	**161**

Comparison of total cash pool and cash management costs

Qualitative parameters

In addition to the above quantitative analysis, qualitative parameters such as;

- rating of the bank,
- commitment from the bank,
- branch network / bank partners,
- technical solutions and assistance,
- service,
- and other for the Group specifically important strategic factors

should be analysed. These factors have to be sorted out and looked at in further detail before making the final decision. If, for example, there is a total discrepancy in how business is made by the bank and the Group, it will probably be difficult to co-operate in the future.

Price is always important, but if the selected set up does not work in practice it does not matter how good the price is. With sophisticated complex international cash pool set-ups the qualitative factors have become the most important selection criteria when selecting a bank for a Group. Once the bank agreement is signed, the Group and its subsidiaries expect an immediate implementation and a perfect bank solution.

When selecting a, totally new bank, for the Group, the commitment from the bank has to be very strong before such a deal can be closed. This should not be the truth only for the first year, but should be a long term commitment not depending on the personnel in the bank.

Before making the final decision, it is advisable to visit reference companies to the banks most likely to be the winner. The reference companies should preferably be using the same type of services as the Group and be the same size concerning number of transactions. When visiting the reference companies, qualitative questions such as back office service, training and implementation skills etc. should be asked and evaluated.

We also recommend a visit to the bank headquarters for payment processing. When paying such a visit, a feeling for the bank will be generated and the answer to a number of still open questions can be retrieved. This visit is an opportunity to study the commitment and professionalism of the bank.

> **The qualitative factors are increasingly important the more complex solutions required by the bank**

Negotiations

The company lawyers should, as mentioned earlier, be introduced already at the vision phase. Now, when the negotiations start, they should also begin to discuss the legal writing in the final contract with the lawyers of the bank most likely to be selected. Particularly when setting up a cross border cash pool solution, there will be many aspects to consider in the contract. Preferably, the legal documentation should be agreed upon before the implementation starts.

By using the spread sheets produced in the previous section, the terms and conditions which needs to be discussed in further detail with the bank can easily be identified.

Decision

After having considered both quantitative and qualitative aspects of the proposals, and made visits to reference customers and the banks, the Group should be ready to make the final decision.

After the decision has been taken, the banks turned down should be informed at once, and a written explanation of why they did not succeed should be given by the Group. The decision should also be communicated as soon as possible internally in the Group. The reasons for having turned down the other banks should also be explained.

Now, the home work is properly done, and the Group is ready to start the implementation phase of the new cash pool and cash management set-up.

SUMMARY AND CONCLUSIONS

Summary

Management philosophy	Input from subsidiaries	Input from banks	Tax and legal	Business case	Final decisions	Production of the RFP	Consolidation and comparison of RFPs	Negotiations	Decision, selection of bank/s	Implementation

Phase 1–Creating the vision   **Phase 2–The RFP and selection of bank**

1. A well founded and accepted vision saves the Group a lot of extra work during the implementation phase.
2. Input from both subsidiaries and banks, tax and legal considerations as well as the creation of a business case are important steps in the process of creating the cash management vision.
3. A well structured and clear RFP saves both the bank and the company a lot of unnecessary work. Therefore, set aside enough time at an early stage to create a well structured RFP.
4. When writing a proposal, it is important for the bank to have a good knowledge about the basic business of the company and its flows. The bank also needs to be open minded and sensitive to the individual requests by the companies, i.e. a proposal has to be tailor made to the individual companies and Groups.

5. References, track record and plans for implementation are important factors in the choice of a new cash management solution.

6. Complex documentation can result in irritation and disbelief in both the concept and the selected bank. There is also a risk for delay of the implementation if the documentation is too extensive and complex.

7. Both quantitative and qualitative factors should be considered when making the final selection of a bank. The Group will be working closely together with the selected bank for a number of years. Therefore, it is important to find a match in the culture of the bank and the company as well as an attractive price level.

Conclusions

Traditionally, proposals used to be difficult to understand. References to general conditions and price lists were common and a thorough explanation of, for example, the electronic banking system was not included. However, recently, the quality of the proposals have slowly improved. At the same time, the companies are working actively to make cash pools and liquidity management more effective and show an increased awareness of the meaning of the different conditions offered by the bank.

All companies are under continuous pressure to cut costs and — on a Group level — work in a more efficient way. For many large Groups there is a substantial savings potential in co-ordinating the Euro cash flow into one total cash pool. The objective for these Groups is to find a solution which will fit into the overall strategy.

The sooner a vision for the concept is created and the bank/banks are selected, the faster the implementation of the cash pool can start. Time is money, what is at stake is a yearly savings potential. Therefore, many companies do not want or cannot afford to wait and see. It will cost them too much.

Töday, international and domestic banks are lining up, eager to do business with profitable companies and Groups. With the pressure to cut costs and to streamline both business and processes, the best and most cost effective solutions are sought.

10

SUCCESSFUL IMPLEMENTATION

INTRODUCTION

Selecting the correct cash management vision is important. So is the choice of banking partner or partners. The previous chapters have dealt with topics which may help you through the steps of assessing your product needs, choosing the appropriate cash pooling vision and selecting your bank partner or partners. The next step is the implementation of your solution. Depending on the sophistication of the solution you have chosen, and the degree of change that this involves for you, this step is probably the longest and hardest one to take in order to reap the benefits of your chosen strategy. This chapter describes the typical steps of implementation and provides you with some hints on how to structure the implementation and, hopefully, how to avoid some of the pitfalls that may lay in your way to successful implementation.

The chapter focuses on large implementation projects, involving several countries and multiple bank products. However, most of the steps of the implementation and most practical opportunities and pitfalls described also apply to smaller and domestic implementations, only on a smaller and less complex scale.

PLANNING YOUR IMPLEMENTATION PROJECT

The most important step of the implementation may be the planning phase. This is when you determine an implementation strategy. There are generally many alternative strategies to choose between, and the best solution for you will depend on your specific circumstances. Based on the strategy choice, the detailed implementation planning follows.

Implementation strategy

A few main strategies to choose between in an international implementation are:

1. The big bang
   Roll out all products in all countries simultaneously.
2. Country by country roll out
   Roll out all products in one country. When you are comfortable that this works, roll out all products in the next country.
3. Product by product roll out
   Roll out one product, such as zero balance pooling, in all countries at the same time. When this is completed, roll out another product across all countries.

In reality, you will probably end up with some combination of these strategies. You may also want to select one or a few countries as pilot countries, where you practice your co-operation with the bank and learn some early lessons before you approach the rest of your countries.

In our experience, it is usually wise to perform the account opening early and across all countries, as this exercise tends to be lengthier than you may expect and can constitute a bottle neck to doing other progress. It is also a process that is preferably carried out in one co-ordinated effort. Read more about this important step of the implementation on page 197 later in this chapter.

If you choose a country by country approach to the product roll-out, you may still want to consider building each interface, for example the automated connection between your accounts payable ledgers and the electronic banking platform, for all countries up front, as it may be more efficient to perform that work with one team which masters the software and the requirements, rather than picking up the interface for amendments each time you roll out another country.[1]

The importance of detailed planning

It is likely that the bank will present you with a high level implementation plan as soon as you announce that you accept their proposal. Be careful to sit down and ensure that this is indeed the way your company wishes to operate. The bank may not be consider fully which other implementation plans you may have, with interdependencies on your bank implementation, such as the implementation of an ERP system or a Shared Service Centre. Expect to put in quite some time up front to create a detailed plan for the implementation. This time is always paid back later in the project if you manage to create a realistic plan which allows you to run the project in a controlled manner. Remember, the dates you commit to in the plan may have very important implications for other parts of the organisation.

---

1 However much you endeavour to streamline your process across countries, remember that the local clearing requirements will be different in each European country!

Example:
The current bulk payments are carried out locally by local staff. The implementation involves migrating the bulk payment process into a Shared Service Centre using new bank technology. When you commit to a migration date, this may mean that the local Finance Director will need to plan for rotating the current payment staff to new positions or, indeed, make them redundant, which requires her to give them notice prior to the production cut-over date to maximise the saving. Your ability to carefully predict which date you will be ready to go into live production will be very important.

A detailed project plan will also enable you to predict the required size and composition of your team over the different phases of the project. Most likely, in the early phases of the project, you will want to involve many key users for process design. Thereafter, you may want to involve a larger proportion of technical resources for the development of interfaces and customisation, and again, towards the latter end of the project, involve more key users for User Acceptance Testing and training activities.

The detailed and credible project plan will be your weapon to defend your resource requirements and allow effective communication with the rest of the organisation. A detailed project plan will also enable you to follow up against actual time spent as the project proceeds and to control and report on your progress as compared to the plan.

This phase is also the time for starting to think about project risks. Read more about risk management on pages 215–221.

THE PROJECT PLAN

Independently of your implementation approach, an implementation plan usually contains a number of basic steps. Below, we have included an example of the typical steps used. This real life example of the implementation of a cash management solution for a newly created shared service centre, contains an account opening and legal documentation activity covering companies in 15 countries and a product roll-out activity including 2 pilot countries for an EB platform, a bulk payment platform and a lockbox facility.

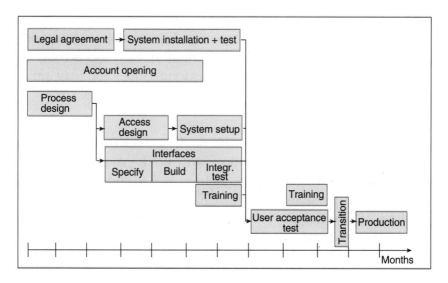

Implementation plan

The phases of the project plan are the following:

1. Legal agreement
   This is the phase when the contract is negotiated. This phase should be completed before actually installing any systems or implementing any products. You will have a much better position for negotiation prior to having tied yourself into the relationship. Read more about this phase on page 193.

2. System installation and testing
   Once the legal agreement is signed, you can install the bank's software and start testing the functionality. Sometimes, if the

legal negotiation takes time, you may be able to pre-process those documents which apply specifically to the software licenses, to enable early installation of the software and thereby winning some time on the critical path. Another solution may be to sign all required documents, but with a side letter explaining that the signature is only temporary and in order to perform some pilot work.

3. Account opening
    The account opening will be more or less complicated depending on the scope of your implementation. Start this activity as early as you can, as it usually takes longer than you may anticipate. Read more about this important phase on page 197.

4. Process design
    As soon as the bank selection is made, the detailed end-to-end process design in co-operation with the bank can start. It is important to design the process from end to end to ensure you cover each possible activity, including, for example, the handling of rejected payments from the bank. Other processes which must be given particular attention in most bank implementations are accounting and bank account reconciliation. The process design is another activity you probably want to complete for all countries at once, to ensure maximum streamlining of the process across all countries.

5. Access design
    Each software implementation contains an element of access design. This is the step when you investigate all the possibilities the software offers and give the right users the appropriate access to the system — but not to any other part of the system. This step is, of course, very important for any software enabling the creation of payment instructions. It can also prove to be rather a complex activity to complete, particularly if users from different areas will use the same software, as is often the case with an EB platform. This is an activity which involves many stakeholders and may require a large portion of co-ordination and management.

Also remember to put in place a secure, but easy to manage, process for on-going access management, to handle the addition of new users and to close the access of users leaving the company or changing positions.

6. System set-up
Most software applications can be configured according to the user's requirements. The system set-up activity is the phase where you set all the various parameters required to support your specific process design.

7. Interfaces
The majority of bank implementations will require the development of one or more interfaces between your previous systems, such as your ERP system or treasury system and the bank systems. Interface development has three main logical steps:
   A. Design, where you specify the functional and technical requirements placed on the interface.
   B. Build, where the interface is technically built.
   C. Integration testing, which you can read more about on page 219.

8. Training
The training activity is usually divided into two parts. First, train the project team and a few key users of the system. This will enable the project team to develop scripts for User Acceptance Testing and the Key Users to execute the test scripts. It will also make it possible to let these Key Users take an active part in training their colleagues at the final training activity, which should take place as close as possible to the date for going into live production, in order that the training may stay fresh in the user's memories.

9. User Acceptance Testing
The User Acceptance Testing is the important phase where the users test the software and accept to take over ownership for their new bank systems. This important activity is further discussed on page 220.

10. Transition

A short time period upon completing the User Acceptance Testing and before going into live production, all transactions on the system must be stopped. During this phase, all the necessary data conversion and other technical preparations for going into live production are performed.

11. Production

Plan for project resources to stay mobilised to support the first few weeks of live production. Regardless of how well you plan, test and train the users, you can be certain that some unexpected surprises will occur, where urgent project team support will be required.

MANAGING THE EXPECTATIONS GAP

During the bank selection process, most banks will have felt pushed into promising functionality and products which may still not be put into production with any other clients. This is particularly relevant at the time of writing this book, where the new Euro currency has recently been introduced and brought with it new product functionality requirements and particularly a user demand for new sophisticated pooling products.

Unfortunately, current market practise is such that the difference between, on one hand, the bank's courting promises and on the other hand, the capabilities actually offered, can be quite large. Therefore, make sure to ask the bank to demonstrate all products offered prior to accepting their proposal. Also ask for several reference visits to other customers of the bank. This may help you form a more realistic opinion of what the bank is able to deliver. If the bank acknowledges not yet having developed a certain product or functionality that you require, but claim it will be delivered at a certain date, demand to see the development plan and obtain the commitment in writing. It is also increasingly common to include penalty clauses in the legal agreement, as regards the timely delivery of implementation.

If you are responsible for the selection of a bank solution, you should make it clear to your sponsor which of the bank's products are more sophisticated and perhaps not used by any other users. Thereby, you will prepare your organisation to handle the expectations gap which can otherwise be a serious risk to your new and sensitive relationship with your banking partner.

Also, make it clear to the bank that you are not taking a naive view to the implementation, but expect the bank to give you realistic planning assumptions and to be frank with you about their actual delivery capabilities. If you are going in to a true, long term partnership relation, it may be quite acceptable that all products or capabilities agreed will not be delivered at once. However, you should demand that the bank provides you, as a partner, with realistic planning assumptions.

PRACTICAL HINTS FOR SUCCESS — AND LESSONS LEARNT

Legal agreement

When the bank choice is completed, you are of course eager to get started with the implementation — reaping the benefits of your laborious selection process. This is when the real frustration usually starts.

The advantage of the large relationship

One of the benefits of implementing a large solution with one banking partner is that you give your company a chance to enter a fair and balanced legal agreement with the bank. If you have relationships with a very large number of banks, it will not be possible to negotiate your transaction banking contracts in any detail, but many companies will tend to sign the banks "general conditions", hardly even reading the small print. Naturally, this contract will be to the advantage of the bank. What is more, when you have more than 20 transaction banking relationships, it will not be humanly possible for anyone in the company to remember what is actually stated in all the contracts you have entered.

In fact, in several companies we have worked with, no contracts are even to be found when we ask to see them. Contracts were entered many years ago, filed by someone who has long since left the company — and the relationship has continued based on good faith and a hand shake at each annual review with the bank.

Entering a large relationship with one bank is your chance to

A) Enter into an equitable legal agreement.

B) Remember what has been agreed, so that you can ensure the agreement is respected.

> **Keeping a small number of large relationships makes it possible to enter equitable agreements – and to remember them**

The last statement is not least important. You may spend days of effort and considerable legal fees to get an equitable legal agreement in place. However, reality is that most of the bank staff that will deliver services to your company will never see that agreement, which will normally end up safely stored away in the legal department of the bank. It is therefore important that key members of your staff, who receive services from the bank, have read the details of the contract and understand its practical implications, so that you can ensure you get value for your money spent on negotiating a good contract. These legal agreements do not only contain liability clauses and responsibility distribution but a fair amount of practical procedures for the day-to-day service delivery!

Legal agreements contain practical procedures

Therefore, it is important that those members of staff who have studied the bank's products and designed the processes for how these products are going to be used, take active part in the negotiation of the legal agreement. Lawyers with expertise in bank law will be required, but the active participation of the "doers" is just as necessary.

Streamlining across countries

When entering an international legal agreement with a bank, you naturally seek to streamline the agreement as far as possible across all the different countries involved. This is difficult, because there is very limited streamlining between the bank legislation in different countries, even within the EMU area. Another difficulty will be to distinguish between what exceptions to the streamlined agreement will be required by law and which will be suggested because they are general local banking practice. We will need to respect those exceptions which are due to differences in local legislation, whereas there is usually no need to complicate your legal agreement by accepting local exceptions based on local practice which the bank is free to step away from in order to give you a more streamlined agreement. In reality, though, local practices in certain countries can be very difficult to avoid. An example of such an area is Germany. It may not be possible, or indeed worth the effort, to persuade the bank to go against the banking community practice in such areas.

Consult a specialist

This is why you will need to solicit the services of a specialist of bank law, preferably belonging to a law firm with a solid international network which can rapidly deliver firm advice and experience in the specialist field of transaction banking. You can trust that the bank will have this expertise on their end of the negotiation table, so you will need the same ammunition on your side to stand a chance of achieving an equitable contract within a reasonable time-scale.

Momentum and project management key to timely completion

These negotiations tend to be lengthy so high momentum in the process will be very important — as the rest of the implementation work will be held up until the contracts are signed. Apart from the sheer volume of contracts to be entered into and the time it takes for all stakeholders to review each redraft, the fact that we are normally dealing with a number of departments and sometimes subsidiaries which may need to be consulted, just as the bank is dealing with a number of branches or divisions, makes very strong project management extremely important in this phase of the project.

Equally important is senior sponsorship, for making the necessary decisions, without delays, to lead the negotiations forward.

You must involve legal expertise, but it is vital for the speed and the budget control of this process that business stakeholders stay very close to the negotiation process. This is to ensure the negotiation moves swiftly away from the more academic points (which may well fascinate the legal advisors on both sides of the table) and concentrates on the important issues.

Proxies to facilitate the process

To avoid the potential complication of gathering signatures on all contracts from all the legal entities which are covered by the legal agreement, it may be worth the effort to gather proxies from these entities, authorising one legal entity to sign on behalf of the rest of the entities involved. Apart from saving administration, you will also avoid the risk of a large number of stakeholders having additional suggestions as to the content of the agreement. Make sure those who should be, are involved in the entire or the relevant parts of the negotiation, but avoid the number of people growing larger than required.

Summary of practical hints — Legal agreement

1. Involve the business stakeholders who understand the practical implications of the agreement

2. Consult a specialist of international transaction banking law

3. Keep a senior sponsor involved for rapid decisions

4. Distinguish between law and local practice

5. Ensure high momentum and strong project management

6. Avoid the academic points and concentrate on business matters

7. Proxies will speed up the process

Account opening

Cumbersome and non-streamlined documentation

Opening new bank accounts for several legal entities in different countries demands a considerable administrative effort. The main reason for this is that each country has its own regulations for what is necessary for the opening of a bank account. On top of that come the more or less cumbersome requirements of your bank to file account opening documentation. A minimum requirement you should place on your international banking partner is that they streamline the documentation required for the purpose of the bank across their different branches. The differences necessary due to local regulations will keep you more than busy.

Most countries will require some sort of proof of company registration. Apart from that, certain countries will require certified photo copies of the passports of each signatory of the company, as an example. Generally, the company will be required to deliver between 3 and 15 different document types for each bank account they wish to open.

Dedicated resource key to success

It is extremely important to take the account opening effort seriously and realise that structure and discipline in the process will be necessary from the start. Do not assume that the back-office manager, for example, will do this with his/her left hand while handling the day-to-day business with the other. Appoint one dedicated person to keep this as his/her main responsibility for the duration of the process. Ensure that this individual has a dedicated support person at the bank, who can co-ordinate the entire process from the bank's point of view. Also, appoint one person in each country/division to co-ordinate all the required documentation from that area, under the guidance of your dedicated account opening co-ordinator.

Do not under estimate the effort

This process often brings to the surface other administrative hurdles. Here is a practical example:

When the signatures on the various documents required are compared to those signatories stated on the registration documents of the company, you may find that the registration document has not been up-dated when the company last replaced a director of a particular legal entity. Thus, to open the account, a new registration document has to be filed with the relevant authority, processed by the authority and returned, before the account can be opened...

In many countries, accounts can be opened prior to each document having been filed, if there is particular urgency. In other countries, this will not be allowed.

Summary of practical hints — Account opening

1. Appoint one person to co-ordinate account opening for all units.

2. Do not expect someone to manage the account opening process with their left hand while managing the day-to-day operations with the other.

3. Do not under estimate the effort and discipline required!

Information technology

Important parts of a bank implementation project is in reality systems implementation. This should be understood as soon as the bank selection process sets out. It is important to involve dedicated IT infrastructure and systems integration resources at the early stages of talking to the banks, ensuring that products are selected, which are compatible with your company's IT platform.

Dedicated systems integration resources

A key to successful implementation is to keep skilled and dedicated IT infrastructure and systems integration resources involved throughout the project. Continuously battling with the rest of the organisation for IT priority will ruin your chances of timely completion and focus your project management efforts where they should not need to be.

Strive for continuity — but document everything

Whilst we strive to achieve as high continuity as possible in the resourcing of a project, in most cases, team members will change over the duration of a large project. Therefore, you must ensure that all project efforts are properly documented. This will enable a smooth transition between team members and also improve the possibilities of maintaining the completed banking system. This is particularly relevant as regards the IT efforts in the implementation project. All technical set-up and development must be properly documented in such a shape that it will be possible to find and to make use of all efforts made.

Communication between users and developers

Key to successful IT development is that business users and developers form effective teams and work together, particularly in the design of the required interfaces. This is one of the reasons we strongly recommend dedicated IT resources throughout the project. Swift and accurate development will depend on access to the business users for review of designs and resolution of queries. This will need to be an iterative process with regular communication. It is important that the business users allocate the priority required to ensure their process design is truly reflected in the design of the interfaces and systems architecture. In our experience from implementation projects, this process works more efficiently when users and developers form teams and develop mutual respect and collegial friendship. The process is also considerably more efficient if professional process analysts participate in the team and help users and developers communicate, by taking on something of an interpreters roll.

Better efficiency in interface development if developers work in the same location

The single most expensive part of a large bank implementation is usually the development and implementation of systems interfaces. Typically, the bank's experts will sit in one location, while your implementation team works on your own premises. Contacts are maintained through telephone and e-mail connections.

Considerable efficiencies can be gained if the investment is made to permit the bank's and your own development resources to work together in the same location. We have experienced instances when delayed interfaces preventing project progress were suddenly rapidly put in place, once the developers from all parties formed a team, rather than being adversaries blaming the non-progress on each other. Remember, the bank's sales team may be an ever so charming group, but the interface designers and builders are not always equally socially skilled.

Safety of electronic banking systems

Many companies make the mistake of believing that a system is secure if you bought it from a bank. "Surely, the bank would not sell you a system which could be broken into? With all the passwords and security features marketed?"

This assumption is as dangerous as it is incorrect. Your system is only as safe as its weakest link. The bank will never guarantee that the way you have installed the system on your networks or PC's will be safe from attempts of fraud, nor that the way you have set up the password configuration will comply with the appropriate standards of segregation of duties. Always ensure your internal audit department reviews your electronic banking systems well before they are put in production.

Summary of practical hints — Information technology

1. Involve dedicated IT resources early in the project.

2. Strive for continuity — but document everything.

3. Communication between users and developers is key to efficient development of interfaces.

4. Better efficiency in interface development is achieved if developers work in the same location.

5. Do not assume a system is secure because you bought it from a bank.

The implementation team

A successful implementation requires the composition of a formal team with clear roles and responsibilities for the team members. How should such a team be shaped and how should it be sponsored?

Project sponsorship

Sponsor

The most important member of the implementation team is probably the project sponsor. To ensure the project gets the attention and resources required and access to swift decisions when needed, the project must have access to a project sponsor with the authority to make the decisions required. The sponsor must therefore, generally, have an important hierarchical position in the organisation, as well as a sufficient understanding of the issues at stake to be in a position to rapidly understand all relevant issues and guide the project in the right direction.

Steering committee

A steering committee should be appointed in each project of any size or importance. The steering committee needs representatives of each major stakeholder group in the project. The steering committee for a bank implementation may consist of the project sponsor, the person who is in charge of bank relationships, perhaps the head of IT, a senior relationship officer from the bank and perhaps a senior executive from a third party vendor involved, such as a partner of a consulting firm involved in the implementation. The role of the steering committee is very close to that of the project sponsor. Whilst the sponsor will drive the project forward and make on-going decisions, the steering committee will meet at regular intervals to resolve any major issues and make the important decisions of the project.

Reference group

It is often beneficial to form a reference group of managers from the business who can ensure that the project delivers that which the business really requires. Regular reviews with the reference group will not only provide the project team with valuable "real world" insight, but also contribute to the buy-in of these important stakeholders. The role of the reference group is to support the project team in achieving its goals.

Project team

The project manager
It is important to recognise that a major bank implementation should never be managed on the side of running a day-to-day business. The project management of a large bank implementation project should be performed by a dedicated resource, with skills not only in cash management and treasury, but also professional training and experience in the skill of project management. The full attention required on day-to-day co-ordination of project efforts, issue resolution, guiding of junior team members, liaison with the company outside of the project etc. is normally a full time job — and should be respected as such.

Key business users
The next group of team members are the key business users. To ensure the project rapidly delivers what the business really needs, the majority of project work should be carried out by skilled users of the end product, who will bring the important practical knowledge of the business to the team. These team members will also play a key role when the new processes are set in production, to train and motivate their colleagues.

IT specialists
We have already mentioned at some length, the importance of the inclusion of IT specialists in the implementation team. After all, a bank implementation project is largely an IT project and the role of these team members must not be ignored.

Team member from the bank
Just as it is an advantage if IT developers from different companies can actually work together, rather than as adversaries, much

frustration can be avoided if the bank can allocate one or more persons to work on the customer site, full time or part time, to become true members of the implementation team, rather than outsiders.

We have found, when various systems are implemented simultaneously, that those system providers which make the investment of allocating implementation support on the client site tend to win much more acceptance in the client organisation than those systems which are supported from a distance. The people-bonding effects should not be under estimated.

Whether the bank can allocate a resource on site or not, your company must always ensure that there is a dedicated implementation manager at the bank, and that you as a customer are satisfied with the quality of that resource. Your project manager will keep daily contacts with that person for extended periods of time.

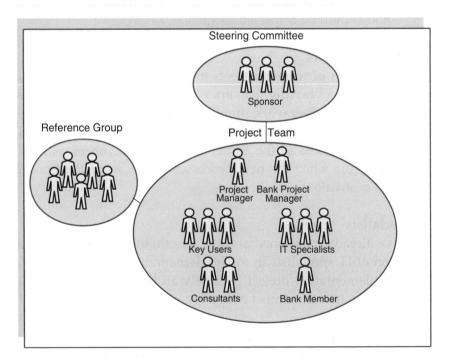

The Successful Implementation Team

Consultants to strengthen the team

Most companies do not have available resources to staff up a large project. Therefore, most large implementations include consultants or other external resources to strengthen the project team. These consultants can serve to support any of the above groups — either a professional project manager, skilled process re-engineering resources to support the key users with methodology skills or experienced IT resource to support the in-house resources.

Usually, the efficiency can be substantially improved by injecting these extra resources into a project. Ensure, however, that none of these roles are entirely dominated by consultants. This is crucial for the continued ownership of the delivered solution, after the life of the project. There must be owners in your own company who know the developed solutions in depth — that knowledge must not be allowed to disappear as your consultants leave the building.

The implementation team

1. Access to project sponsor with authority to make decisions.

2. Steering committee for issue resolution and project steering.

3. Reference group to support the project team.

4. Dedicated, professional project manager.

5. Key users to provide business knowledge.

6. IT specialists.

7. Team members from the bank.

8. Consultants to strengthen the team.

STAKEHOLDER COMMITMENT

Without commitment, no change effort will ever be successful. How do we achieve the commitment of the various stakeholders involved in a bank implementation project? There is, of course, no up-the-sleeve magicians trick for this. Below are a few examples of how we approach the issue of commitment in relation to a few vital groups of stakeholders.

The banks we are leaving

Changing cash management banks is not done overnight. This process will last for at least several months and often a number of years. This means that you will need to handle the relationship with the banks which you are leaving very carefully — while performing the selection process and while going through the implementation phase of your project. Throughout this period, your company will depend on the co-operation from and relationship with those banks.

Proactive communication

The first thing to remember is to communicate regularly and as frankly as possible with these banks. Make sure you offer them the opportunity to take part in the selection process. In some cases, you know from the start that a particular local bank will not have any chance of qualifying in your selection. You should then contact a senior relationship manager and explain why you will need to look for cash management services from other banks. Most likely, this will be because his bank is not offering the sort of products you are seeking. The local bank will normally accept this argument and appreciate you giving the true reasons you are reducing this business with them. Importantly, ensure the banks you will be leaving receive the news from yourselves and not from a third party!

> **Ensure the banks you are leaving receive the news from yourselves and not from a third party**

The First Steps of Communication

1. Draft an easy to read communication message in "question and answer" form to be distributed from the bank project to all local Finance Directors, outlining the message of which change is expected to take place in your bank relationships, the reasons for this and the expected timing. This is to ensure your local officials have all the information they will need to feel comfortable, but also to ensure a consistent and correct message is being communicated.

2. The local Finance Director contacts the local bank/banks and gives them an early warning that the Group's bank relationships will change, but that the bank will be kept informed each step of the way.

3. Arrange for a joint visit to each bank by a senior representative from the headquarters along with the local Finance Director. Show the bank the respect to come out and talk to them in person, whilst displaying that the matter is now out of the hands of the local manager (if, indeed, that is the case). This will also provide support to the manager, who may not be as close to the bank implementation project as the headquarter representative and might feel uncomfortable explaining to an old business contact that a good relationship is about to change character.

Transaction banking is not your only banking business

Another successful strategy to make sure you get the commitment and loyalty from your old banking partners that you will need throughout the implementation, is to find means to give these banks more business — but other than your bank account and money transfer business. For example, you may be in a position to tell them: "We will reduce the volume of supplier payments and customer receipts with your bank, but we intend to increase the money market and foreign exchange volumes instead."

> **"We will reduce the volume of supplier payments and customer receipts with your bank, but we intend to increase the money market and foreign exchange volumes instead"**

New bank and system vendors

Demand understanding of the complete change situation

A large bank implementation is normally a complex operation involving several different system vendors (i.e. your ERP vendor, the vendor of your treasury system, perhaps the vendor of an independent electronic banking platform) and a large number of bank service users (perhaps the different groups in a shared service centre: Payables personnel, Receivables personnel… and local users at your international branches.) In order to manage a project of that size and complexity, you will need to follow a rigid, but logical, project plan where business requirement identification precedes bank selection and where process design precedes interface development and user training. The bank will, of course, need to be involved in the process design, as regards the best way to integrate the bank's products and facilities in the corporation's business support processes.

It is therefore astonishing to find how often the bank will send a training professional to a client site without previously briefing him/her of the process which has been agreed for the use of the bank's software at that particular client site. Instead, the trainer may well teach the users all the various ways he can use the software, ignoring the process design which has previously taken place in co-operation between the corporate customer and the bank.

A minimum requirement to place on the bank's Implementation Manager is that each person who arrives on the client site, be it for technical support or training purposes, is properly briefed on the specific client situation.

More on site co-operation gives better dynamics

The more time the bank's Implementation Manager spends on the customer site as a true team member, the higher the likelihood for a smooth implementation where bank staff and customer staff work together to progress the project and to resolve issues which arise. The cost to the bank is probably off-set by the improved overall project progress and improved dynamics. One of the biggest challenges in implementation work is to avoid an "us-and-them" culture, threatening the important relationship between the partnership bank and the customer in this early and sensitive stage.

Dual Implementation Sponsorship

Ensure the Senior Relationship Officer as well as the committed Sales Officer from the bank are part of the implementation Steering Committee. Whereas the implementation officers assisting you with the implementation may have a more "cost avoidance" view of the world, the business representatives of the bank are more likely to support rapid implementation of the service delivery. These representatives will also have the same knowledge of the recent selection process as you do, and it may, from time to time, be necessary to remind them of promises made during the courting process.

What else can you do to motivate the bank to succeed?

Another way to increase the bank's incentive to prioritise your implementation may be to investigate opportunities to help the bank be successful by making you successful. You may propose to the bank that you publish an article in a trade magazine about your successful implementation, or perhaps give a presentation together with the bank on a conference visited by target customers of the bank. Of course, you can only agree to do these things if you are as happy with the service as you expect to be, and you must retain your integrity to give a balanced opinion of how the bank's service has really been delivered.

Thus, in order to ensure the commitment of the chosen bank:

1. Demand proper client pre-briefing of all bank personnel involved in your implementation.

2. Ensure bank and customer personnel work as a team.

3. Involve senior business sponsors from the bank in the implementation Steering Committee.

4. Help the bank to be successful by making you successful.

Local stakeholders

Communication

Local users of bank services will need to be involved as early as possible in the bank selection stage. Therefore, it should not be any surprise to them when the implementation starts. However, to ensure you get these important stakeholders on your side in the implementation, keep them closely involved in the implementation progress, explaining *why* things will need to change — in certain locations things may not change for the better, but it will be for the better from a Group point of view. Explain exactly *what* will happen and *when* it will happen. Ensure your plans are aligned with those of the local branches. Avoid making visits to a branch at the time of their month end close, for example, when they will be busy with other tasks than your project.

To ensure this important communication does not start ambitiously to later on be forgotten or ad hoc, it may be a good idea for the project to publish a regular Bank Implementation News Letter distributed to all stakeholders, updating them on progress in the project, any changes to plans or design, or introducing people who are involved.

Just as it is usually appropriate for a senior project member or project sponsor to make a road show to the local banks, it may be necessary for the same person to set up specific meetings with local management to explain the rational behind the project and to communicate the senior commitment behind the bank implementation project. Certain local managers are more than likely to oppose the change and special attention may be required to get these involved and committed to the project. If this happens, it is time for the sponsor to step in and support the project team, which should not be left alone to handle that sort of in-house issues.

Project participation

The best way to gain the commitment from local stakeholders is to involve them as much as possible in the project. There are primarily two roles during the implementation where you are likely to involve them, as members of a Reference Group or as Key Users in the project team.

The role of the Reference Group is to support the project team with local process knowledge and to function as a reality check on the proposals presented by the project team. Of course, they are also the customers of the project team, and as such, must communicate their needs on delivery from the project.

Key Users in the project team are actively involved in the process design. They also provide the business input to the interface design and prepare realistic scripts for system testing. They monitor the system testing to ensure the results produced are correct and they manage or execute the user acceptance tests. They will also participate in training their colleagues to use the new bank tools and processes when each part of the project is set in production.

The benefits of involving local stakeholders in the project in this way are obvious. First, they will provide valuable knowledge, vital for the success of the project. Second, their involvement will reduce most resistance from other local stakeholders. If colleagues who they know and trust have actually been involved in the project, they will feel more comfortable with the result.

A word of warning when recruiting for project teams...

Of course, there is always a risk when you ask for in-house project resource. It is unlikely that any managers will send you their strongest people — more likely you may receive a warm recommendation for someone they wanted to see the back of for some time...

This is a real problem, as it will not only undermine the work products and efficiency of the implementation team, but also reverse the desired confidence building effect of involving someone who is trusted by his/her colleagues.

Try to recruit the people you have had previous and successful contacts with and be prepared to take swift action if you identify you have been allocated the wrong individual.

Headquarter stakeholders

Communication

The headquarter stakeholders have a lot in common with the local stakeholders. They, too, may experience change resistance, having to move from well known tested processes to a new bank with new processes and new systems. On top of that, they are more than likely to experience more change than many of the local stakeholders. Particularly in the cases where the bank implementation is a part of the creation of a Shared Service Centre or the implementation of an ERP-system. The main rule for communication to headquarter stakeholders is similar to that for communication to local stakeholders: Communicate *why*, *what* and *when* there will be change.

The important thing to remember is that whilst the headquarter stakeholders may be close to the change, you must not take it for granted that they have been communicated "the bigger picture" by someone else. To a user of the new electronic banking platform it may not at all be clear why there is a need to change banks. "The old system worked perfectly well. Why change?" Remember to clearly communicate the reasons the change is necessary. Perhaps you desire to implement a new bulk payment product, which was not provided by your former headquarter bank. Remember to communicate these reasons to everyone involved.

Also, be extra careful to provide these stakeholders with information of the longer term implementation plan. As these Users are likely to be the ones who are the most exposed to change, they are also the most likely to be struck by change fatigue. Mitigate that risk by preparing them mentally that you are entering into a long period of development, where gradual change will take place. Inform them up-front that your project plans are your best estimate to date and that they should be prepared that these plans may change as the project proceeds and new facts become known. Prepare them for a long but interesting time together and point out all the advantages that the project holds for them, such as the possibility to learn and work with best practice processes and the latest available banking technology. Encourage them to participate where they can in the project and to learn as much as possible from the implementation experience, a valuable opportunity that is likely to be useful in their continued careers.

Ownership

Involve as many Users as possible directly in the execution of the project. If the project lasts over several years, take the opportunity to roll different people in and out of the project, to enable as many as possible to feel personal ownership of the project and the new tools made available to the Users. The gradual build-up of ownership with the Users is a key to successful production.

Usually, there is a gradual hand-over of ownership to users following the following steps:

- Key Users participate in process design, facilitated by the project team.

- Key Users, who are members of the project team, prepare the scripts for the Conference Room Pilot (CRP). In Conference Room Pilot sessions, the project team demonstrates the system functionality to the End Users, who may ask questions and query whether or not their specific requirements can be met.

- Key Users provide business specifications for interface development and verify the interface testing results.

- The second to last step prior to setting the new systems in production is User Acceptance Testing (UAT). The test scripts will be prepared by Key Users who are members of the project team, but the tests are executed and signed off by End Users. By signing off a script, they acknowledge that the system will respond to their business requirements and that they are comfortable that the functionality will be satisfactory.

The last step before setting the system in production is End User training. This should be executed, as far as possible, by those Key Users which have participated actively in the project, supported by the bank's training experts.

This gradual hand-over of ownership from the project team to the users should not only be limited to the use of the various electronic banking tools, but also to the bank relationship. The day-to-day production relationship is one between various users in the organisation and a vast range of staff from the bank. The project team must ensure that the appropriate introductions are made between the relevant people–that names and telephone numbers of the key support officers for various services provided by the bank are distributed–and that the appropriate escalation procedure in case of a problem is in place–prior to going live with the new processes and banking platforms.

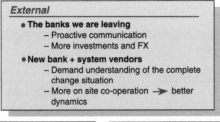

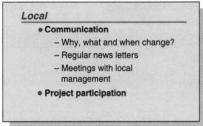 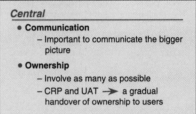

How to obtain Stakeholder Commitment and Support

RISK CONTROL

Any project contains a number of risks. Risks are of varying nature. For example, there are risks to the quality of the project and there are risks that the project may be delayed. This section discusses a few ways in which you can operate in order to control and manage the risks of your bank implementation.

Risk and issue management

At the start of the project, the project manager should sit down and think about all the things which may possibly go wrong throughout the project. Also, consider which impact each negative event would have and if it is likely to happen or not. Further, develop a strategy for what you can possibly do to avoid that the negative event occurs and last, develop a contingency strategy, i.e. what you will do if the adverse event occurs.

Document these risks in a risk charter. Here is an example of how this might look.

#	Risk	Impact	Probability	How to avoid	Contingency
1	The legal review of the bank contract may not be delivered on time.	This would delay the completion of the legal agreement. That would delay the installation of the EB platform and the account opening.	High	Liaise regularly with legal counsellor.	Sign those documents which are required for installation of EB platform, but with a rider explaining that the agreement is of temporary nature and will be re-opened for negotiation upon completion of legal review.
2	Interface between AP ledger and bank may not be ready for the planned production day.	This would delay the production start.	Low	Monitor development closely. Ensure early review by key user.	Keep current payment process with current bank.
3					

Risk charter

This way of structured thinking should help you control the risks and to manage those events which will, regardless of how well you manage the project, come up during the project. The project manager should keep the risk log updated throughout the project and regularly distribute it to the steering committee.

The next simple project management tool which is commonly used in most implementation projects is the issue log. The issue log is the project manager's tool for monitoring and, when required, escalating issues which may hinder the progress of the project. The issue log should be very regularly updated and reviewed within the project team at least once a week and reviewed each time the steering committee convenes. Here is an example of a typical issue log.

#	Issue	Impact	Raised by	Date	Action	Respon-sible	Due date	Status
1	French lockbox users unable to spend required time on resolving outstanding design issues.	User requirements on French lockbox interface incomplete.	Andy Baker	05-05-00	Liaise with French key user Edith Piaf.	Charles Brown	10-05-00	Open
2	Law firm has not delivered legal opinion on time.	Legal negotiation delayed by at least six weeks.	Dawn Brindle	08-05-00	Sign documentation with rider.	Bill Shake-speare	15-06-00	Open
3								
4								

Issue log

A well managed issue log will ensure that issues are swiftly dealt with and that every issue gets the appropriate attention.

Documentation and sign-off

Documentation of work products

In every project of some duration, there will be some rotation of project members. To make those transitions as smooth as possible, it is important that each work product in the project is well documented, using proper version control. This is also important for future development which may be required.

Physical acceptance signature on each project deliverable

Many of the key users and other persons with positions of responsibility will be very busy during project times. To ensure that you get the proper attention and commitment from these important people, you should ensure that each work product of significance gets physically signed off by the person who is responsible for reviewing and agreeing its content.

This is primarily a way to ensure you get commitment at the right time. There is a risk that an interface design gets reviewed and agreed by the user. It is built based on the design. When the user is later asked to sign off the test, he tells you that, in fact, the design was wrong and the interface will need to be amended. If he is asked to take formal responsibility for signing off the design, it is more likely that the design error will be picked up earlier and at a much smaller cost.

The second reason is that these signatures are a way for the project team to ensure responsibility is assigned to the right people. Without a proper sign-off procedure, the likelihood is higher that it is the project team which will be solely blamed if the project is delayed, when often the responsibility for delays rests with individuals who may not be within the direct control of the project team.

Test, test and test again

As we have said before, an important part of most larger bank implementations of today is related to the implementation of IT solutions. Therefore, your implementation plan must include structured and thorough testing of each piece of software which is implemented. Below is a brief overview of the basic test steps you probably want to go through.

Typical phases of testing

1. Conference Room Pilot

   In Conference Room Pilot, the standard configuration of the new software is demonstrated to the key users which are given the opportunity to raise questions referring to their specific functionality requirements. The demonstration is based on scripts, which should replicate the process design for the specific corporation. Thus, the Conference Room Pilot sessions take place after the completion of the process design work.

2. Unit test

   In unit tests, each piece of development, be it interfaces or customisations of the software, is tested in isolation. These tests, too, should be performed based on scripts containing realistic data.

3. Integration test

   At the integration test phase, the different parts of the software solution are tested together. This means that each type of transaction is allowed to flow through all parts of the software it will actually require in live production. The same scripts are followed throughout the chain of systems and, of course, the end result is carefully checked against the expected, scripted, result.

   This is the phase of testing where you may also include volume testing of the software solution, i.e. passing peak time volumes of transactions through the software, including any connectivity device, to ensure the solution will actually handle the capacity you are anticipating. If you can perform the volume test based on your live data, this will be a chance to simultaneously test if your data cleansing activities have been successful.

Example of volume and data cleansing test:
The current bulk payment method of our client was in-house cheque printing. We wanted to start sending all bulk payments as electronic instructions to the bank, through a bulk payment product. First, we gathered all bank account numbers from all suppliers and entered these in our customer data base. To test the cleanliness of the data, we passed test payments including all bank account numbers through the bank's payment test environment. Thus, we could pick up any bank account numbers which were rejected by the bank's test protocol, prior to actually making live payments, whilst simultaneously testing the volume capacity of the system.

4. User Acceptance Test

   In User Acceptance Tests, the end users execute scripts to test the functionality of the system. This is the last testing step prior to going into live production. When the users have signed off the Acceptance Test, they have accepted that they are prepared to take over the ownership of the system from the project team.

Ensure a common format of *Process Design, User Acceptance Test scripts* and *Procedures Manuals.* This will save considerable effort in the production of these documents!

Fall back procedures

Well ahead of going into live production with your new bank systems, you should consider what to do, if, despite your thorough testing process, the system does not work properly when you go live. This is what we call fall back procedures.

The fall back procedures should be part of your risk matrix (see above). Many fall back procedures will not only be required for the time immediately after production cut-over, but will be relevant for the ongoing production.

Example of a typical fall back procedure:
The main procedure is that every financial payment is sent through the new EB platform.

If, for any of many possible reasons, the EB platform does not function, payments should be sent with fax instruction, followed by a call back procedure, to verify that the fax is not fraudulent.

It is important that this procedure is well known to each user from the day of going live, and that the current list of persons authorised to issue the fax instruction is readily available, as must be the list of persons the bank may call back for verification.

As payments are often sent close to the cut-off time, the non-availability of the EB platform may be discovered late and, as most readers are aware, penalties for late financial payments can be costly. Therefore, the switch over to fall back procedure must be swift and simple to perform and must never rely on the availability of one key person, or a project team, who holds on to all the non-standard information.

Summary of key points to remember about risk control in implementation projects

1. Analyse and document all known risks in a risk charter.

2. Keep an issue log to manage and escalate all relevant issues.

3. Document all work products.

4. Ensure each project deliverable is signed off by the responsible person.

5. The typical phases of testing are: Conference Room Pilot, Unit test, System test and User Acceptance Test.

6. Ensure fallback procedures are in place and well known by the End Users before going into live production.

INDEX